❧ The Literary Garden ❧

❧ The ❧
Literary Garden

WITH AN INTRODUCTION BY
DUNCAN BRINE

Illustrated by Lea Richardson and Jesse Kaplan

A Lark Production

B
BERKLEY BOOKS, NEW YORK

B

A Berkley Book
Published by The Berkley Publishing Group
A division of Penguin Putnam Inc.
375 Hudson Street
New York, New York 10014

This book is an original publication of The Berkley Publishing Group.

PRINTING HISTORY
Berkley hardcover edition / March 2001

The Penguin Putnam Inc. World Wide Web site address is
http://www.penguinputnam.com

Library of Congress Cataloging-in-Publication Data

The literary garden / with an introduction by Duncan Brine ; illustrated by Lea Richardson
and Jesse Kaplan.—Berkley hardcover ed.
        p.   cm.
    A collection of excerpts from classic fiction, along with related gardening,
cooking and craft articles, and original illustrations.
    "A Lark production "
    Includes index.
    ISBN 0-425-16874-3
    1. Gardens—Literary collections. 2. Gardening—Literary collections.   I. Brine, Duncan.

PN6071.G27 L57 2001
808.8'0364—dc21
                                                    00-069889

PRINTED IN THE UNITED STATES OF AMERICA

10 9 8 7 6 5 4 3 2 1

 CONTENTS 

CONTENTS

CONTENTS

CONTENTS

CONTENTS

CONTENTS

CONTENTS

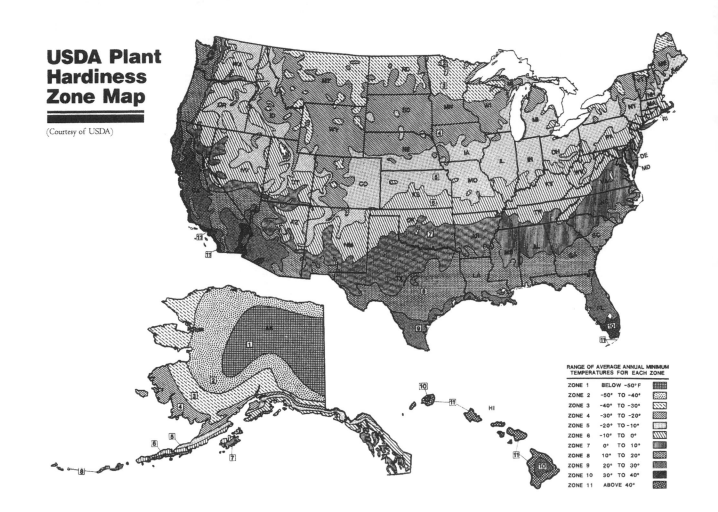

USDA Plant Hardiness Zone Map

(Courtesy of USDA)

RANGE OF AVERAGE ANNUAL MINIMUM TEMPERATURES FOR EACH ZONE	
ZONE 1	BELOW −50° F
ZONE 2	−50° TO −40°
ZONE 3	−40° TO −30°
ZONE 4	−30° TO −20°
ZONE 5	−20° TO −10°
ZONE 6	−10° TO 0°
ZONE 7	0° TO 10°
ZONE 8	10° TO 20°
ZONE 9	20° TO 30°
ZONE 10	30° TO 40°
ZONE 11	ABOVE 40°

To determine your growing zone, consult the map above. Plants can survive in zones greater or equal to their minimum hardiness zone, which is usually indicated on plant labels. It is important to know your zone and stick to a plant's hardiness rating guidelines— no matter how skilled or enthusiastic the gardener, there's just no tricking Mother Nature.

❧ INTRODUCTION ❧

When a writer imagines a garden, he asks his reader to make a leap with him. He invites the reader to see the rose or smell the scent of magnolia. The reader is more than willing to go along. What if we tried to turn a garden of words into an actual living garden?

There is a great distance between fantasizing about a novelist's garden and growing it. *The Literary Garden* helps bridge that gap. An appealing mélange, this book is a collection of passages from classic fiction alongside related gardening, cooking, and craft articles, as well as original illustrations. From Conrad Aiken to Émile Zola, these passages provide a collective vision of the "why" of gardening. We are enthused and encouraged when we recognize these great authors—among them Cather, Fitzgerald, Hawthorne, Sandburg, and Wolfe—are truly gardeners at heart.

We are introduced to an archetypal garden. This garden is often a formal space, a walled garden. It's a stage within which a drama unfolds; life is heightened and exalted. Expressions are exaggerated; pleasures are focused. We recognize this garden as universal, though each author personalizes it with intimate images. Brontë's garden is ". . . Eden-like . . . full of trees, it bloomed with flowers: a very high wall shut it out . . . ." Hugo writes in *Les Misérables:* ". . . impenetrable as a forest, populous as a city, tremulous as a nest, dark as a cathedral, odorous as a bouquet, solitary as a tomb, full of life as a multitude." Hawthorne gives us Rappaccini's lush garden, where a nearly operatic "fall" occurs.

In *The Literary Garden*, no element is more evocative or uniquely characteristic than fragrance. Brontë writes: ". . . my step is stayed—not by sound, not by sight, but once more by a warning fragrance. Sweet briar and southernwood, jasmine, pink, and rose, have long been yielding their evening sacrifice of incense . . ." And who can forget the forbidding fragrant lilac in *Dorian Gray?*

Fragrance is, perhaps, the most powerful and pervasive theme threading these literary excerpts together. A natural scene is set once the scent is conjured. Characters abandon themselves to the atmosphere. It is fragrance that transports the characters and the readers to a place that is emotional rather than physical. It is not the walls of the garden or even its plants that move us, but the fragrant air between them.

We enjoy it when authors put faces on plants. Baum provides a double-dose of anthropomorphism when his Cowardly Lion observes that *he* likes flowers which "oft seem so helpless and frail." And Alcott's roses, ". . . rejoicing with all their hearts, . . . with . . . their ruddy faces . . . whispering to one another" and peeping through windows while others wave and offer tribute "to the gentle mistress who had loved and tended them so long." In Lewis Carroll's garden Alice exclaims, "I *wish* you could talk!" And the Tiger-Lily responds, "We can talk! . . . when there's anybody worth talking to."

Gardeners and authors want different things from their gardens, although their worlds and wishes cross-pollinate. A gardener's garden is all too real, menaced by pestilence, drought, and other enemies. For an author, the garden is a more perfect, idealized place created to illuminate character. The garden mirrors—externalizes—a character's inner self.

Gardeners are grateful to have the garden to relieve the drudgery of everyday existence. We need the garden and recognize the garden's need for us. The garden cries out for care—"The beans are dying, the tomatoes are clamoring for me, the peas are holding out their hands!"—and we happily acquiesce.

The Literary Garden engages our imagination. It's as likely to make the reader run to the library and borrow *Look Homeward, Angel* as it is to inspire him to get in the garden and dig. We're encouraged to think of roses not just for cutting but also for making rosewater and rose-petal garni. Cather's *My Ántonia* prompts anticipation of harvesting our own pumpkins or making pumpkin pasta. Sherwood Anderson compels us to invite bees into our backyards to make our gardens more productive.

This book provides enchantment and instruction. The passages inspire us to read more and garden more. The illustrations depict the gardens the authors have imagined. The directions and recipes are an impetus to build, create, cook, and plant.

Fiction is the driving force, as old interests are rekindled and fresh discoveries inspire us to pursue new interests. You will hardly be able to resist the impulse to get out and garden.

Duncan Brine

Pawling, New York

"The Dark City"

His greatest pleasure in life came always at dusk. Its prelude was the reading of the evening paper in the train that took him out of the city. By long association the very unfolding of the grimy ink-smelling sheets was part of the ritual: his dark eyes dilated, he felt himself begin to "grin," the staggering load of business detail, under which he had struggled all day in the office, was instantly forgotten. He read rapidly, devoured with rapacious eyes column after column—New York, London, Paris, Lisbon—wars, revolutions, bargains in umbrellas, exhibitions of watercolors. This consumed three-quarters of the journey. After that he watched the procession of houses, walls, trees, reeling past in the mellow slant light, and began already to feel his garden about him. He observed the flight of the train unconsciously, and it was almost automatically, at the unrealized sight of a certain group of trees, oddly leaning away from each other, like a group of ballet dancers expressing an extravagance of horror, that he rose and approached the door.

The sense of escape was instant. Sky and earth generously took him, the train fled shrieking into the vague bright infinity of afternoon. The last faint wail of it, as it plunged into a tunnel, always seemed to him to curl about his head like a white tentacle, too weak to be taken seriously. Then, in the abrupt silence, he began climbing the long hill that led to his house....

He turned the corner and saw his house before him, riding on the hill like a small ship on a long green wave. The three children were playing a wild game of croquet, shrieking. Louder sounds arose at his appearance, and as he strode across the lawn they danced about him chattering and quarreling.

"Daddy, Martha won't play in her turn, and I say—"

"Marjorie takes the heavy mallet—"

The chorus rose shrill about him, but he laughed and went into the house, shouting only, "Out of the way! I'm in a hurry! The beans are dying, the tomatoes are clamoring for me, the peas are holding out their hands!"

"Daddy says the beans are dying. Isn't he silly?"

"Let's get to the garden before daddy does."...

He ran out of the side door, under the wisteria-covered trellis, and down the slippery stone steps to the vegetable garden.

"Here comes daddy, now," shrilled to him from Martha.

He lighted his pipe, shutting his left eye, and stood in profound meditation before the orderly, dignified, and extraordinarily vigorous rows of beans. They were in blossom—bees were tumbling the delicate lilac-pink little hoods. Clouds of fragrance came up from them. The crickets were beginning to tune up for the evening. The sun was poised above the black water-tower on the far hill.

Martha and Marjorie began giggling mysteriously behind the lilacs.

"My hoe!" he wailed.

The hoe was thrust out from behind the lilacs.

"If anybody should drive up in a scarlet taxi," he said to Martha, accepting the hoe, "and inform you that your soul is free, don't believe him. Tell him he's a liar. Point me out to him as a symbol of the abject slavery that all life is. Say that I'm in a miserable thrall to wife, children, and beans— particularly beans. I spend my days on my knees before my beans."

"I'll do nothing of the sort," said Martha....

He sighed, and for a moment rested his chin on the hoe-handle, peering out towards the tree-encircled swamp. The hylas were beginning to jingle their elfin bells. A red-winged blackbird sailed in the last sunlight from one apple-tree to another.

"All a vicious circle—and all fascinating. Utterly preposterous and futile, but fascinating."

He dropped the hoe and trundled the wheelbarrow to the edge of the strawberry-bed.

"Why can't you stay where you're put?" he said. "Why do you grow all over the place like this?"

With a trowel he began digging up the runners and placing them on the wheelbarrow. It delighted him to part the soft cool soil with his fingers, to thrust them sensitively among the finely filamented roots. The delicate snap, subterranean, of rootlets gave him a delicious pang. "Blood flows—but it's all for the best; in the best of all possible worlds. Yield to me, strawberries, and you shall bear. I am the resurrection and the life." When he had a sufficient pile of plants, he trundled the wheelbarrow to the new bed, exquisitely prepared, rich, warm, inviting. With the hoe he made a series of holes, and then, stooping, thrust the hairy roots back into the earth, pressing the soil tenderly about them. Then he rose, stretched his back, and lighted his pipe, shutting his left eye, and enshrining the flame, which danced, in the hollow of his stained hands. The cloud of smoke went up like incense.

"Water!" he cried. "Water! Water!"

Martha appeared, after a moment, bringing the watering-pot. She held it in front of her with both hands.

"Quick, Martha, before they die. Their tongues are turning black."

"Silly!" Martha replied.

The earth about each plant was darkened with the tilted water, and the soiled leaves and stems were brightened.

"Listen, daddy! They're smacking their lips."

"They are pale, they have their eyes shut, they are reaching desperately down into the darkness for something to hold on to. They grope and tickle at atoms of soil, they shrink away from pebbles, they sigh and relax."

"When the dew falls, they'll sing."

"Ha! ha! what fools we are."

He flung the hoe across the wheelbarrow and started wheeling it towards the toolhouse.

"Bring the watering-pot."

Martha ran after him and put it in the wheelbarrow.

"That's right—add to my burden—never do anything that you can make somebody else do."

Martha giggled in response and skipped towards the house. When she reached the stone steps she put her feet close together and with dark seriousness hopped up step after step in that manner. He watched her and smiled.

"O Lord, Lord," he said, "what a circus we are."

He trundled the bumping wheelbarrow and whistled. The red sun, enormous in the slight haze, was gashing itself cruelly on a black pine-tree. The hylas, by now, had burst into full shrill-sweet chorus in the swamp, and of the birds all but a few scraping grackles were still. "Peace—peace—peace," sang the hylas, a thousand at once. Silver bells, frailer than thimbles, ringing under a still and infinite sea of ether…

"Peace—peace," he murmured. Then he dropped the wheelbarrow in horror, and put his hands to his ears. "The enemy!" he cried. "Martha! hurry! Martha!" This time Martha seemed to be out of earshot, so he was obliged to circumvent the enemy with great caution. The enemy was a toad who sat by preference near the toolhouse door: obese, sage, and wrinkled like a Chinese god. "Toad that under cold stone." Marvelous compulsion of rhythm…

He thrust the wheelbarrow into the cool pleasant-smelling darkness of the toolhouse, and walked towards the kitchen door, which just at that moment Hilda opened.

"Hurry up," she said. Her voice had a delicious mildness in the still air and added curiously to his already overwhelming sense of luxury. He had, for a moment, an extraordinarily satisfying sense of space.

The Commuter's Solace

NOWADAYS IT IS not enough to call oneself a gardener; you must be prepared to make a distinction that allows others to know, at a word, the purity of your commitment to the garden. You can be an heirloom gardener, a window box gardener, an organic gardener, an armchair gardener, a weekend gardener, and even a twenty-minute gardener!

To be a commuter gardener, however, may be the most honorable of all gardening distinctions, as it suggests an esteemed work ethic that carries over into the garden. The commuter gardener knows that no matter what the hour, no matter how little light is left at the end of the day, the work of the garden must be done. And while this work is not a chore, it is a responsibility to which the commuter gardener willingly submits.

The commuter gardener is efficient, above all else. Tasks are tended in the tiniest corners of a day, carefully timed to be in sync with the sun, the soil, and the train schedule. The yard and garden are mentally carved up so that all can be managed piecemeal, this patch before breakfast, that one after dessert. And weekends are left for the massive undertakings such as wholesale tilling or building and setting the frame for a raised bed. Some of this breed look forward to getting lost in the disappearing light of dusk and leave weeding to the cool of the evening. Others steal moments to water or prepare the soil for planting in the wee hours at dawn.

For the commuter gardener, all of this time in the garden is stolen, snatched away from the other priorities that clamor for attention before or after hours: family, meals, reading, household chores. This clamor is barely audible to the commuter gardener, though, for he has found his solace in the seedlings and flowers and fruits that come from the bits and pieces of time and trouble he spends on his garden.

CONRAD AIKEN

❧ On My Knees Before My Beans ❧

GREEN BEANS ARE one of the most productive and trouble-free garden crops. They can even be cultivated in containers on an urban patio. Green beans (of the genus *Phaseolus*) fall into two general categories: pole and bush. Each kind offers varieties that produce beans of different shape, color, and size.

Also called runner beans, pole beans are known for their choice flavor, long growing season, and high nutritional value. They are easier to pick than bush beans, but require more labor and cultivation. The vertical climbing supports that hold their lengthy vines conserve space, making them ideal for small gardens. Common supports, such as a trellis, pole, or teepee, add whimsy and interest to the garden. Simply wrap a rough string around the supports to encourage the sensory hairs of the vines to twine. The teepee is especially fun for children: Lay a bed of straw in the center of the structure to create a shady hideaway.

An economical way of growing pole beans is by creating tower trellises of five-foot-wide wire mesh, the type used to reinforce concrete. Buy about sixty feet for five trellises, and then use wire cutters to divide it into twelve-foot lengths that will be rolled into hoops. Fasten the ends together with short lengths of narrow-gauge wire and stand the support on end.

Wait until after the last frost to sow pole bean seeds, placing them an inch or two deep and two to three inches apart in well-prepared, manured soil. If planting on a trellis, sow seeds along the base of the supports in rows three to four feet apart. If using poles, plant six seeds at the base of each. After the plants sprout, thin them to three plants per pole.

Some common varieties include the Kentucky Wonder, Case Knife, Blue Lake, Musica, Kentucky Blue, and Ramona.

Bush beans are easy to cultivate and allow for early harvesting. They are full of rich flavor and produce a full yield in a short period of time. They're relatively disease-free, though they are vulnerable to the predations of animals and mildew, and mud. As with the pole beans, sow seeds one or two inches deep and two to three inches apart, but place them in short rows eighteen to thirty-six inches apart. To increase the yield, plant successive crops every ten days through August.

A twenty-five-foot row will yield more than enough for a family of four, and using the staging method will produce enough beans for freezing to eat during the winter.

Favored bush varieties include Bush Blue Lake, Tendercrop, Topcrop, Nugget, Blue Lagoon, Jade, and Greensleeves.

Bean plants are shallow-rooted, so cultivate carefully. Regular watering is critical when the plants are in flower and will increase yield. The crop will need at least a quarter-inch of water each day during dry periods, but avoid wetting the foliage. Keep the plants thinned to six inches and spread mulch to prevent weeds and plant rot.

Careful watering will help prevent the diseases bean plants are susceptible to. And a dusting of Rotenone will help stave off Mexican bean beetles (which look like yellow ladybugs) and bean weevils. Organic controls are also available.

As soon as two weeks after flowering, the beans are ready to be picked. They can be snapped off at any time, but once the seeds start to swell, the crisp texture and taste begin to fade. Keep the plants well picked to extend the harvest and boost production. When the harvest is over, discard the old plants and prepare for a new crop.

All bean varieties can be enjoyed canned, frozen, pickled, or dried. Tiny, fresh beans are a tender gourmet treat.

The Enemy!

A TOAD AS the enemy? The opposite is surely true. But for his odd looks, a toad can be a significant addition to any garden. Sure, a lump of a creature hopping out into the garden path can frighten the unsuspecting gardener, but that's a small price to pay for having a toad in the garden. As mysterious and ugly as they may be, keeping toads around is indisputably beneficial.

Think of it. Toads aren't the only creepy things hanging around the garden. Slugs, beetles, and other bugs are none too pretty themselves. And *they're* destructive, devouring precious plants, grinning with every bite. A beetle is happily munching a leaf when suddenly, a dark mass approaches. In a split second, the beetle is gone. Now, it's the toad that's grinning. A toad's diet consists mainly of garden pests. Unappetizing to us, perhaps, but beneficial to our little patch of growing things.

Saving a tomato crop is surely worth having a toad or two, but pest control is just one of the toad's many talents. Who would have thought a toad can help aerate the garden? Sometimes a toad needs to find a dark, moist hideaway from the summer sun. He just digs himself a little hole in the garden soil and hides out until sundown. Meanwhile, the soil has gotten a burst of fresh air from the toad's digging. Think of the toad (as well as his good friend, the earthworm) as an air and soil circulation manager. In goes the toad with the fresh air, then out goes the toad with the stale air. A couple of tasty garden pests are all he requires in payment. Not a bad deal at all for any gardener.

Finally, a toad truly can add an interesting aesthetic quality to any garden. Those little stone figurines one finds in many garden shops cost money. A toad is free. Think of him as a little living gargoyle. Patiently waiting until the next bug crawls by, he is a fine example of living art. Two seconds later, he hops over a row of plants, and then he becomes a piece of performance art. What gardener could ask for more?

Toads may not be pretty, but they really should be given a welcome home in the garden. Gardens are places of function and beauty. Give a toad a chance, and in his own way, he'll add generously to both.

CONRAD AIKEN

✿ Rampant Strawberries ✿

STRAWBERRIES CAN BE grown virtually anywhere in the United States. Many new virus-free varieties have been developed for parts of the country where survival of the plants used to be sketchy at best. With a little planning, proper planting, and care, home gardeners can benefit from these developments and harvest plentiful, tasty strawberries of their own.

Planning for strawberries entails two decisions: what kinds to plant and where to plant them. Strawberry plants come in two basic types: June bearers produce the earliest fruit, usually in June and early July, and ever-bearers, which fruit in both summer and fall. Some good June bearers to try are Robinson, Guardian, Surecrop, and Allstar. Everbearers like Ozark Beauty, Tristar, Tribune, and Sparkle will produce berries through late autumn. Combining both types in the garden will ensure a good harvest throughout the entire season.

In deciding where to plant, remember that the strawberries will remain in the chosen spot for two or more years, so find a nice area with full sun and designate as much space as is manageable in the garden. Strawberries propagate by runners—shoots from an original "mother" plant that run across the ground, take root, and produce "daughter" plants. This method of propagation can create an unruly strawberry patch if not watched carefully.

The two basic planting plans for strawberries are the hill system and the matted row. The hill system does not call for an actual hill; rather, the name describes how the plants look in the garden. Single plants are spaced twelve to fifteen inches apart. This method is especially good for small gardens where long rows of plants aren't practical. For larger areas, be sure to keep a walkway between the plants about every four feet for care and harvesting. With the hill system, the runners are never allowed to grow into new plants. They are cut as soon as they appear, keeping only the single original plant growing. These plants grow large and lush, creating the look of small hills of plants in the garden. The advantage to this method is that the energy usually used in growing runners is channeled into growing larger berries.

A matted row plan is just that—a row of plants allowed to grow and propagate to form a thick mat of greenery. A little more space is needed for the rows, but less care is required since the runners are allowed to grow into new plants. Space the plants about eighteen inches apart, with three feet between rows. When the runners appear, steer them toward the plants on either side to fill in the area between them. Take care to avoid overcrowding, as this will result in smaller berries. The advantage to growing strawberries in a row is that when older plants need to be replaced, there are plenty of other plants nearby to fill in the gaps and continue bearing fruit.

Plant strawberries in a sunny spot in well-drained soil enriched with manure or compost. The root system is shallow, so all water and nutrients must be available in only a few inches of soil. Plant in the early spring, as soon as the danger of hard frost is over. The plants should be placed in the hole with the crown at ground level—never below the soil. Fan the roots out, cover with soil (avoiding getting any on the plant), and water immediately.

Care of strawberry plants is simple: Keep them moist and weed-free. Mulch placed around the plants will keep much-needed moisture in the soil and discourage weeds. Use straw, hay, wood chips, or leaves to cover the ground between plants. In the winter, cover the plants entirely with mulch to prevent any damage. When spring rolls around, simply move the winter mulch cover between the plants.

For the best berries and strongest plants, pinch the blossoms from the plants the first year. For ever-bearing varieties, pinch off only the first summer blossoms and allow the autumn blossoms to grow. Replace strawberry plants at intervals over the years to keep a full fruit-bearing patch.

Keeping an eye on the strawberries will ensure a healthy, bountiful harvest year after year. Plan it, plant it, and care for it—the keys to a successful strawberry patch.

Little Women

The June roses over the porch were awake bright and early that morning, rejoicing with all their hearts in the cloudless sunshine, like friendly little neighbors, as they were. Quite flushed with excitement were their ruddy faces, as they swung in the wind, whispering to one another what they had seen; for some peeped in at the dining-room windows, where the feast was spread, some climbed up to nod and smile at the sisters as they dressed the bride, others waved a welcome to those who came and went on various errands in garden, porch, and hall, and all, from the rosiest full-blown flower to the palest baby-bud, offered their tribute of beauty and fragrance to the gentle mistress who had loved and tended them so long.

ELEGANT ROSES RAMBLING over housefronts, walls, trellises, fences, and arbors create a fragrant and charming atmosphere. Climbing roses—a good choice for small as well as large gardens—assure a vibrant, lively presence; contrasting backgrounds enhance their beauty. Cottage gardeners of eighteenth-century England so admired these exquisite plants that they raised the cultivation of its genus, *Rosa*, to a new art form. Lavish displays of cascading blooms continue to thrive in gardens all over England.

Still, many gardeners shy away from growing roses, fearing the plants will require too much time and care. But this isn't the case; many growers offer both heirloom varieties and new cultivars that are hardy, vigorous, and disease-resistant. They require little attention, so the gardener can spend more time enjoying these "little neighbors" instead of cultivating them.

Rose specialists consider climbers and ramblers two separate groups, but they share several characteristics. Ramblers produce clusters of small flowers on strong stems that grow from the base of the plant; they bloom for a season then must be cut back to the quick. Climbers produce strong stems from any part of the plant, allowing for more height and bloom potential; they flower from their original shoots for two or more seasons

LOUISA MAY ALCOTT

before pruning is required. A thoughtful selection of plants can ensure a season of continuous bloom.

To plant roses, select a site that enjoys at least half a day of full sun and has well-drained soil. Dig a deep hole close to the intended support and work in generous amounts of compost, rotted manure, and peat moss. Mound the soil and carefully place the rosebush on the top and drape the roots evenly. Then, mix additional amounts of the compost, manure, and peat into the remaining soil and shovel it around the bush until the hole is completely filled. Water liberally and apply a two-inch covering of mulch. Keep in mind that the canes will need to be firmly secured to the support. Wait to fertilize until after the plant has become established.

In the spring, prune climbers by cutting back the lateral flowering shoots to two or three buds. Ramblers should be pruned by cutting flower-bearing stems back to ground level immediately after the flowering is complete.

It is always wise to check with the local garden center for varieties that grow best in specific climates. Popular varieties include:

Climbers: Constance Spry, William Baffin, Mary Wallace, Aloha, Mermaid, Mme Gregoire
Staechelin, New Dawn
Ramblers: Paul's Himalayan Musk Rambler, Bobbie James

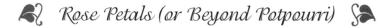

Rose Petals (or Beyond Potpourri)

THE ROSE HAS been regarded as the queen of flowers since the dawn of gardening; equally long has been man's attempt to capture the rose's delicious scent well after the flower has faded. The use of rose water, for instance, dates from as early as 2,000 years ago. Wealthy Romans bathed in rose water and used roses for everything from soothing stomachs to curing hangovers. Indian cuisine incorporates rose water, as do many Middle Eastern desserts. After all, that's what makes a Turkish Delight delightful.

Rose water is actually simple to make. Pour a half cup of boiling water over one cup of fragrant and fresh rose petals. Let it steep for fifteen minutes, then strain and store in the refrigerator to prevent mildew. This can be used alone as an after-bath splash or mixed half-and-half with vegetable glycerin to make a body lotion. Combine a half cup rose water with three tablespoons vegetable glycerin for a refreshing toner. Use rose water with French clay to make a wonderful face mask. Both vegetable glycerin and French clay are available at health food stores. Luxuriate in a bath scented with rose water and feel the power of the roses that captivated the ancient Romans.

Roses adapt to the kitchen beautifully. Rose water can be used to provide the essence of rose in many desserts. Used in small quantities, it can provide that wonderful taste that is not quite recognizable but adds a hint of richness to the dish. Sprinkle a tablespoon of rose water over apple pie filling before putting on the top crust and baking. Use a bit in homemade ice creams, pastry creams, or cake fillings.

Rose petals can be used as a garnish or scattered over a salad for a refreshing change. Wash the petals gently, then thoroughly dry before using. Candied rose petals make beautiful additions to any dessert plate. Dip petals in stiff egg whites, then in extra fine sugar (using tweezers helps with this). Place on waxed paper to dry. Store them layered in waxed paper in an airtight container. When using rose petals for edible garnishes and rose water in food, be sure to only use roses that have not been sprayed with any garden chemicals.

So the next time you cut a few roses for a bouquet, set aside a couple of blooms and experiment with the petals' other pleasant uses.

Winesburg, Ohio

In imagination he saw himself putting his arm about her waist and feeling arms clasped tightly around his neck. One of those odd combinations of events and places made him connect the idea of love-making with this girl and a spot he had visited some days before. He had gone on an errand to the house of a farmer who lived on a hillside beyond the Fair Ground and had returned by a path through a field. At the foot of the hill below the farmer's house Seth had stopped beneath a sycamore tree and looked about him. A soft humming noise had greeted his ears. For a moment he had thought the tree must be the home of a swarm of bees.

And then, looking down, Seth had seen the bees everywhere all about him in the long grass. He stood in a mass of weeds that grew waist-high in the field that ran away from the hillside. The weeds were abloom with tiny purple blossoms and gave forth an overpowering fragrance. Upon the weeds the bees were gathered in armies, singing as they worked.

Seth imagined himself lying on a summer evening, buried deep among the weeds beneath the tree. Beside him, in the scene built in his fancy, lay Helen White, her hand lying in his hand. A peculiar reluctance kept him from kissing her lips, but he felt he might have done that if he wished.

Instead, he lay perfectly still, looking at her and listening to the army of bees that sang the sustained masterful song of labor above his head.

The Army of Bees

WHEN BEES MAKE a garden their home, fruits and vegetables become more luscious, and flowering plants thrive. The secret: The bees drink the nectar and carry away the pollen used to fertilize your plants and trees. Beekeeping can be done virtually anywhere in the United States. It doesn't take much to get started—just some research, a supplier, and an adventurous spirit.

Read books and journals or watch videos about beekeeping to familiarize yourself with the process. Take advantage of beekeeping organizations in your area. Seek out a local beekeeper and set aside a summer afternoon to watch how he tends the bees. Experienced beekeepers can be an invaluable source of tips and advice about your bees. And don't forget to check your state regulations about beekeeping. Some states require registration with the Department of Agriculture.

A smart way to begin is to buy new equipment and packaged bees. In putting together the equipment, the new beekeeper learns how it works and gets an idea of how the bee colony will live. Starting with packaged bees allows the beginner to learn how to handle a hive from its birth. Buying an already established hive can cause control problems for a novice. Be sure to purchase equipment and bees from a reputable source: ones found in a beekeeping magazine or someone recommended from a local organization.

Plan to buy the equipment in the winter to allow time to get familiar with it before the bees arrive. Select a beginning "hobby kit" that includes all the parts of the structure where the bees will live and produce honey. It should also include a smoker and some basic honey harvesting equipment.

The bees should be ordered to arrive in the early spring—order them early (usually when ordering your equipment) to make sure the supplier can meet the time frame. The three most common types of bees ordered are the Italian, Carniolan, and Caucasian. Each has advantages and disadvantages—consult a local beekeeper on which type is best for your area. Bees come in two- to three-pound packages, delivered in a crate. One package is one hive of bees; it will include a queen, worker bees, and drones. While more costly, the larger packages are usually better for the beginner as the bees can establish themselves more quickly. Although the survival rate of new hives is very good, some like to purchase enough equipment to start two hives of bees. That way, if one queen dies, the two hives can be merged instead of losing everything and having to start over again next year.

Bees should be kept in the package until everything is ready for installation. Keep them fed by sprinkling sugar water (one part granulated sugar to one part warm water) until they don't take any more. Keep them in a cool, dry, and dark area before installing. They can be held in their shipping package for up to twenty-four hours, though the sooner the package is installed, the better. Place the bees into the hive in the late afternoon or early evening, following the instructions provided in the package or from a bee manual. This gives them a chance to get organized and become familiar with the area before flying out to forage during the day.

Safety is an obvious concern with beekeeping. While bee stings are usually just an annoyance, which the beekeeper soon becomes almost immune to, if you are allergic to bee venom, beekeeping may not be for you. Safely tending the bees means wearing the right clothing and having the right equipment. Your clothing should be light colored and made of cotton. Dark colors and wool fabrics tend to anger the bees and make them difficult to manage. Protective face netting and long leather gloves are recommended for beginners. The smoker included in your beginner's kit helps calm the bees during other beekeeping chores. It turns the bees back into the hive to eat, and bees with full stomachs are easier to work with.

Looking for that perfectly ripe peach, the most beautiful begonia, or a drop of honey for your tea? The bee can do it all. The buzz on beekeeping is that it's a relaxing hobby that will benefit and enrich your garden.

Additional Information

American Bee Journal, Dadant and Sons Inc., Hamilton, IL 62341

ABC and XYZ of Bee Culture. A. I. Root, E. R. Root, H. H. Root, and J. A. Root. Medina, Ohio: A. I. Root Co., 1975.

First Lessons in Beekeeping. Dadant and Sons, eds. Hamilton, IL: Charles Scribner's Sons, 1980.

The Joys of Beekeeping. Richard Taylor. New York: St. Martin's Press, 1974.

Bee Gardens

NOT EVERYONE HAS the ability or desire to keep bees, but anyone can create a garden that will attract wild bees. The insects will pollinate the plants and trees, leaving the fruits, vegetables, and flowers large and lush. Bees need to eat the nectar from flowers to produce the honey stored in the hives. While collecting the nectar, the pollen in the flowers sticks to their legs, and the bees carry it away to another plant or tree and fertilize it.

Bees are color sensitive, so use visual cues. Plant white, blue, and yellow blossoms for the best luck. Use the annuals and perennials that naturally grow in the area: As bees already feed off these native plants, it will be like serving up their favorite flowers. Most local nurseries will carry the native plants or seeds to start the garden. Even dandelions will attract bees. For a luxurious bee pasture, fill a large area with sweet clover, goldenrod, and fireweed.

To keep the bees around, provide them an area where they can nest. Many types of bees nest underground, so leave a patch of bare ground near the garden. Bees find it hard to nest in manicured lawns, so the small empty space will be just right. Bees also nest in dead trees and branches filled with beetle burrows. If a dead tree is too much to keep on the property, take a couple of dead branches, drill varying-sized holes in them, and hang them around the garden or shed. Even scrap wood will do. Into a piece of wood, drill holes three to five inches deep without going through the wood completely. Nail this securely in a protected place such as under the eaves of a garage or shed. Nests should be near water, like a small pond, a birdbath, or an old bucket kept filled with fresh water.

SHERWOOD ANDERSON

Honey Grog

WHY SHOULD THE bees be the only ones enjoying the honey? This natural sweetener has become a popular substitute for refined sugar in many recipes. Whether it comes from raising your own bees or from the supermarket shelf, honey is a natural choice for sweetening almost anything. Mix up a batch of this honey grog and be enveloped by the soothing taste of nature's nectar.

4 cups apple cider or apple juice
¼ cup honey
2 tablespoons butter
1 cinnamon stick
1 teaspoon grated orange peel
¼ teaspoon freshly ground nutmeg
½ cup light rum (optional)

Combine all ingredients, except rum, in a saucepan and bring to a simmer, stirring occasionally. Simmer for five minutes. If desired, stir in rum just before serving.

YIELD: 8 servings

The Country Doctor

They went through the dining-room, and reached the garden by way of a sort of vestibule at the foot of the staircase between the salon and the dining-room. Beyond a great glass door at the farther end of the vestibule lay a flight of stone steps which adorned the garden side of the house. The garden itself was divided into four large squares of equal size by two paths that intersected each other in the form of a cross, a box edging along their sides. At the farther end there was a thick, green alley of hornbeam-trees, which had been the joy and pride of the late owner. The soldier seated himself on a worm-eaten bench, and saw neither the trellis-work nor the espaliers, nor the vegetables of which Jacquotte took such great care. She followed the traditions of the epicurean churchman to whom this valuable garden owed its origin; but Benassis himself regarded it with sufficient indifference.

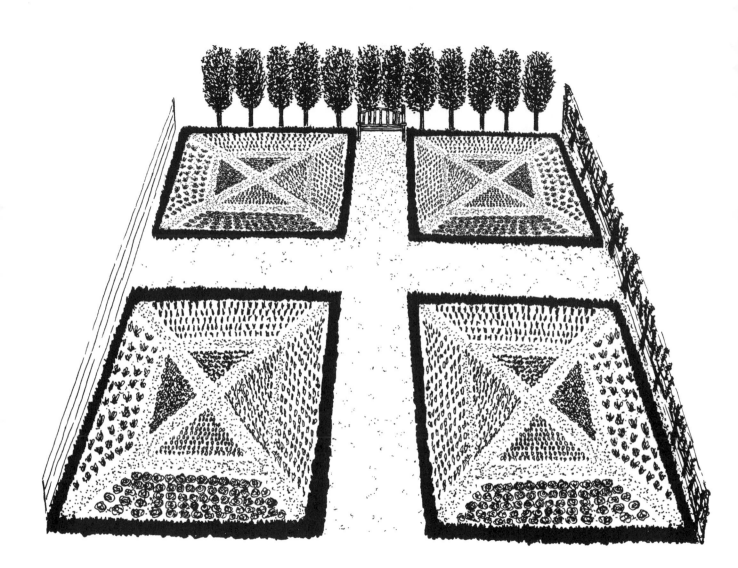

The Churchman's Garden

THE SOLDIER MAY have been indifferent to his surroundings, but Jacquotte knew she was being rewarded by the effort of her garden's previous owner, the churchman. She "followed the traditions of the epicurean churchman to whom this valuable garden owed its origin"—she lovingly picked up where he left off as a gardener.

There are many times in a gardener's life when he is able to or must start from scratch. Indeed, pride causes a gardener to want to forge his own path, to create his own unique and unmistakable impression in the garden. But some of the greatest delights are found in the inherited bits of garden one encounters over a lifetime.

Say you move to an old house whose environs have not been kept up, but it is clear the grounds were once the realm of a true gardener. The clues are everywhere: the perfectly situated, statuesque oak trees that shade the open face of the house; the scraggly roses that still hug both sides of the back porch; the scores of tender shoots that appear in the spring, whether or not anyone's watching. Perhaps there are long-empty raised beds or the makings of a grape arbor, long abandoned. But the bones of a garden someone once loved are there.

Don't be in a rush to make a big mark. Even as you're getting started making plans and making changes in your yard, spend the first season looking for the ghosts in your garden. Look for ways to benefit from the gifts of the gardeners who preceded you. If the early garden was intelligent and lovable, as was the churchman's garden, go with it, adapt it, make it your own. If there's not much to work with, look for some small way to honor the history of the earlier garden. Perhaps bring back to its previous glory an old lilac that has stopped flowering from neglect. Or add your own favorites to an ancient bed of bulbs. Even the tiniest nod to the gardener who dug before you keeps the thread of gardening history intact.

HONORÉ DE BALZAC

THE EUROPEAN HORNBEAM (*carpinus betulus*) is truly a four-season tree. From its delicate green leaves in summer to its twiggy gray silhouette in winter, the hornbeam adds color and interest to any landscape.

Native to Europe and common there for centuries for making hedges and allees, the hornbeam is hardy in climate Zones 5 to 9. In spring and summer, its dark green leaves set off the smooth, slate-gray bark. In the fall, the leaves turn yellow, providing a pleasant show. Although bare of leaves in the winter, the gray bark on the trunk and branches contrast beautifully with snowy landscapes.

A cousin of the birch, the hornbeam is a slow-growing tree, about a foot per year, a characteristic that makes it suitable for small yards or patios. However, over the years, it can reach twenty or thirty feet. Of particular interest for hedging and narrow upright screens is the cultivar Columnaris, which grows to 35 feet, but only 6 feet wide.

The hornbeam may be difficult to find in a nursery, as it usually isn't requested often enough to warrant stocking them, and can be fairly difficult to transplant. If you can't find them locally, they can be special-ordered to arrive in time for spring planting.

The only requirement for a thriving hornbeam is that it be planted in well-drained soil. The tree is virtually pest-free and unlike similarly shaped trees such as the poplar, is long-lived and requires little maintenance. The hornbeam is a particularly good choice any time you need a living fence in the garden.

The Espalier

AN ESPALIER IS any tree or shrub trained to grow from its natural bushy, three-dimensional shape into a flat, two-dimensional shape. While not difficult, it does require considerable time, patience, and diligence; the result, however, is a spectacular form of natural art.

Espaliers are trained to grow against a wall, fence, or trellis, the plant's branches being pruned and guided into a design of the gardener's choosing. The simplest design is the single stem or cordon. This allows only one main branch to form in either a vertical or a diagonal direction. More challenging designs include the candelabrum (shaped just as the name suggests) and the Belgian fence (requiring five or more plants trained into an interlocking diamond pattern). The more informal types of espaliers include the free form, which follows the plant's natural shape, and the fan, which allows the branches to fan out in a more natural form.

Your intention for the space will define which plant material to use for espaliers. Fruit trees, such as the apple or pear, lend themselves beautifully to this approach. Not only are they attractive, but they can bear exceedingly bountiful crops of fruit for up to thirty years. Cherry and plum trees are also common espaliers, but they are a bit more difficult to work with. If the gardener doesn't want to use a fruit tree, a flowering dogwood makes an especially beautiful espalier. Among shrubs, cotoneaster and pyracantha bushes are often espaliered to highlight their attractive berries and growth habits.

Growing an espalier requires some sort of a support. A wall that can accommodate a system of ties for training the espalier is perfect. If not, a trellis placed in front of the wall can support the plant and the ties. A fence makes a handy support, and the espaliers will end up providing additional coverage. Espaliers are trained with proper pruning—not only to eliminate unwanted branches but to guide the existing branches into proper shapes. Commonly, bamboo stakes are tied to the branches and anchored by ties to the support. This encourages straight growth, allowing for a more precise design.

This artistic and distinctive gardening technique will allow even the smallest of gardens to support an espalier: the actual design is limited only by your imagination. With a bit of commitment, anyone can transform an ordinary wall or fence into a piece of art.

HONORÉ DE BALZAC

ESPALIER DESIGNS

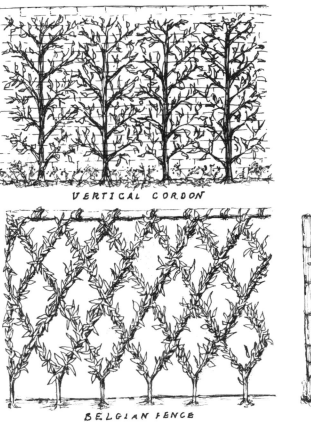

VERTICAL CORDON

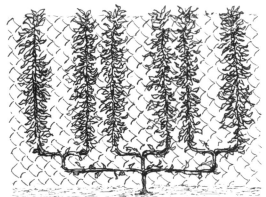

CANDELABRUM

BELGIAN FENCE

FAN

They walked along listening to the singing of the brightly colored birds and looking at the lovely flowers which now became so thick that the ground was carpeted with them. There were big yellow and white and blue and purple blossoms, besides great clusters of scarlet poppies, which were so brilliant in color they almost dazzled Dorothy's eyes.

"Aren't they beautiful?" the girl asked, as she breathed in the spicy scent of the bright flowers.

"I suppose so," answered the Scarecrow. "When I have brains, I shall probably like them better."

"If I only had a heart, I should love them," added the Tin Woodman.

"I always did like flowers," said the Lion. "They oft seem so helpless and frail. But there are none in the forest so bright as these."

They now came upon more and more of the big scarlet poppies, and fewer and fewer of the other flowers; and soon they found themselves in the midst of a great meadow of poppies. Now it is well known that when there are many of these flowers together their odor is so powerful that anyone who breathes it falls asleep, and if the sleeper is not carried away from the scent of the flowers, he sleeps on and on forever. But Dorothy did not know this, nor could she get away from the bright red flowers that were everywhere about; so presently her eyes grew heavy and she felt she must sit down to rest and to sleep.

But the Tin Woodman would not let her do this.

"We must hurry and get back to the road of yellow brick before dark," he said; and the Scarecrow agreed with him. So they kept walking until Dorothy could stand no longer. Her eyes closed in spite of herself and she forgot where she was and fell among the poppies, fast asleep.

"What shall we do?" asked the Tin Woodman.

"If we leave her here she will die," said the Lion. "The smell of the flowers is killing us all. I myself can scarcely keep my eyes open, and the dog is asleep already."

It was true; Toto had fallen down beside his little mistress. But the Scarecrow and the Tin Woodman, not being made of flesh, were not troubled by the scent of the flowers.

"Run fast," said the Scarecrow to the Lion, "and get out of this deadly flower bed as soon as you can. We will bring the little girl with us, but if you should fall asleep you are too big to be carried."

So the Lion aroused himself and bounded forward as fast as he could go. In a moment he was out of sight.

"Let us make a chair with our hands and carry her," said the Scarecrow. So they picked up Toto and put the dog in Dorothy's lap, and then they made a chair with their hands for the seat and their arms for the arms and carried the sleeping girl between them through the flowers.

On and on they walked, and it seemed that the great carpet of deadly flowers that surrounded them would never end. They followed the bend of the river, and at last came upon their friend the Lion, lying fast asleep among the poppies. The flowers had been too strong for the huge beast and he had given up at last, and fallen only a short distance from the end of the poppy bed, where the sweet grass spread in beautiful green fields before them.

"We can do nothing for him," said the Tin Woodman, sadly; "for he is much too heavy to lift. We must leave him here to sleep on forever, and perhaps he will dream that he has found courage at last."

"I'm sorry," said the Scarecrow. "The Lion was a very good comrade for one so cowardly. But let us go on."

They carried the sleeping girl to a pretty spot beside the river, far enough from the poppy field to prevent her breathing any more of the poison of the flowers, and here they laid her gently on the soft grass and waited for the fresh breeze to waken her.

ONE OF THE brightest flowers of the garden, the poppy is sweetly scented and easy to grow. The poppy, or *Papaver*, genus includes the opium poppy, which is famous for its narcotic qualities, as well as many other purely decorative varieties. Poppies will grow as true annuals as well as perennials grown as annuals, since they last only two or three years. Poppies need to be sown each season to maintain their dazzling presence in the garden. There are varieties available for every zone.

Large, brilliantly-colored, cup-shaped flowers begin to appear in early spring and are noted for their crinkly crepe paper texture, black-stained centers, golden stamens, and whiskery stalks. Common flower colors include shades of pink, red, orange, and pure white. Garden poppies are excellent cut flowers and should be clipped when the bud swells but before the flower opens. After cutting, seal the ends with hot water or flame to prevent the sap from running out; the bloom will last longer.

Poppies deliver the most spectacular effect when massed together in beds. Popular types include Alpine, Tulip, Iceland, and Shirley. Transplant small plants in the fall for spring blooms, or sow seeds in the fall or spring in a spot that enjoys full sun and light, well-drained, average garden soil. Mix a handful of seed with fine, dry sand and scatter or plant in rows. A light covering of mulch will help keep the soil cool and the roots moist. Thin the emerging plants in early spring, spacing them six to twelve inches apart. Water in the

morning to help prevent disease. If the stems grow too high, staking may be required. Deadheading flowers will encourage blooming.

Poppies can be propagated by root cuttings or division, but neither is necessary. The plants will happily remain in their appointed place for the duration of their life in the garden. The division method is a quicker way to produce more plants. Since the roots are extremely sensitive, division can only be done after the foliage dies back in midsummer. Dig up a clump and divide it into groups about four to six inches across. Replant twelve to fifteen inches apart in enriched soil.

Poppies are susceptible to aphids and northern root knot. Use an insecticide soap to eliminate them.

Welcome these fanciful blooms into the garden. Their alluring beauty will seduce the most experienced gardener.

Jane Eyre

It was now the sweetest hour of the twenty-four: —"Day its fervid fires had wasted," and dew fell cool on panting plain and scorched summit. Where the sun had gone down in simple state—pure of the pomp of clouds—spread a solemn purple, burning with the light of red jewel and furnace flame at one point, on one hill-peak, and extending high and wide, soft and still softer, over half heaven. The east had its own charm of fine, deep blue, and its own modest gem, a rising and solitary star: soon it would boast the moon; but she was yet beneath the horizon.

I walked a while on the pavement; but a subtle, well-known scent—that of a cigar—stole from some window; I saw the library casement open a hand-breadth; I knew I might be watched thence; so I went apart into the orchard. No nook in the grounds more sheltered and more Eden-like; it was full of trees, it bloomed with flowers: a very high wall shut it out from the court, on one side; on the other, a beech avenue screened it from the lawn. At the bottom was a sunk fence; its sole separation from lonely fields: a winding walk, bordered with laurels and terminating in a giant horse-chestnut, circled at the base by a seat, led down to the fence. Here one could wander unseen. While such honey-dew fell, such silence reigned, such gloaming gathered, I felt as if I could haunt such shade for ever: but in threading the flower and fruit parterres at the upper part of the inclosure, enticed there by the light the now-rising moon casts on this more open quarter, my step is stayed—not by sound, not by sight, but once more by a warning fragrance.

Sweet briar and southernwood, jasmine, pink, and rose, have long been yielding their evening sacrifice of incense: this new scent is neither of shrub or flower; it is—I know it well—it is Mr. Rochester's cigar. I look round and I listen. I see trees laden with ripening fruit. I hear a nightingale warbling in a wood half a mile off; no moving form is visible, no coming step audible; but that perfume increases: I must flee. I make for the wicket leading to the shrubbery, and I see Mr. Rochester entering. I step aside into the ivy recess, he will not stay long: he will soon return whence he came, and if I sit still he will never see me.

But no—eventide is as pleasant to him as to me, and this antique garden as attractive; and he strolls on, now lifting the gooseberry-tree branches to look at the fruit, large as plums, with which they are laden; now taking a ripe cherry from the wall; now stooping towards a knot of flowers, either to inhale their fragrance or to admire the dew-beads on their petals. A great moth goes humming by me; it alights on a plant at Mr. Rochester's foot: he sees it, and bends to examine it.

"Now he has his back towards me," thought I, "and he is occupied too; perhaps, if I walk softly, I can slip away unnoticed."

I trode on an edging of turf that the crackle of the pebbly gravel might not betray me: he was standing among the beds at a yard or two distant from where I had to pass; the moth apparently engaged him. "I shall get by very well," I meditated. As I crossed his shadow, thrown long over the garden by the moon, not yet risen high, he said quietly without turning:—"Jane, come and look at this fellow."

I had made no noise: he had not eyes behind—could his shadow feel? I started at first, and then I approached him.

"Look at his wings," said he, "he reminds me rather of a West Indian insect; one does not often see so large and gay a night-rover in England: there! he is flown."

The moth roamed away. I was sheepishly retreating also; but Mr. Rochester followed me, and when we reached the wicket, he said:—"Turn back: on so lovely a night it is a shame to sit in the house; and surely no one can wish to go to bed while sunset is thus at meeting with moonrise."

🌿 The Gooseberry Bush 🌿

GOOSEBERRIES WERE FIRST cultivated in Europe in the thirteenth century, and quickly became a revered part of almost every garden. Settlers brought them to America early on but for some reason the gooseberry never really caught on in the United States. However, people who grow them now say they couldn't live without them.

There are two types of gooseberry bushes: the European and the American. European varieties often don't grow well in the United States because of their susceptibility to mildew. American varieties are hardier, require little care, and can withstand the colder American winters.

There are three different colors of gooseberries. The red varieties, such as Poorman and Red Jacket, are the sweetest. They are good to eat right from the bush or to use in fresh desserts. The pink varieties, like Pixwell and Welcome, are less sweet and are good for pies and jams or eating fresh when they are completely ripe. Downing and Oregon are green-fruited types. These are less sweet and perfect for pies and jams. Gooseberry bushes can be quite thorny, making the fruit difficult to pick: Poorman and Welcome varieties are less so than most.

Gooseberry bushes are available from a number of sources. Mail-order catalogs or local nurseries carry many common varieties. One thing to keep in mind when purchasing the bushes is that many states have regulations about growing gooseberries. Like their cousins the currants, they can sometimes harbor white pine blister rust, which can be a serious problem in areas where

CHARLOTTE BRONTË

forestry is important. Although the problem is not as widespread as it used to be, some states still require a license to grow gooseberry bushes. Check your local agricultural department for any planting restrictions in your area.

Planting and caring for the bushes is relatively easy. Plant them in the spring, as soon as the ground is thawed. Gooseberry bushes are not picky when it comes to a garden spot. Direct sunlight or partial shade will do. In areas where the summers are particularly warm, the bushes should be planted in partial shade for best results. Space the bushes about four feet apart. Mulch with manure, sawdust, or hay to retain moisture.

Gooseberry bushes don't require much pruning. The first year after fruiting, prune back to the six strongest branches. After that, prune any branches that are three years old or more to about fifteen branches. This will result in more and larger berries.

Buying disease-free stock from a nursery will ensure a good start for the gooseberry bush. Although relatively disease-free naturally, some varieties can be susceptible to powdery mildew. To combat this, prune the bush to allow air circulation throughout, especially where bushes are planted in partial shade. Aphids can also be a problem, causing the leaves to turn brown and curl. Pick off affected leaves and burn them, or, better yet, try introducing ladybugs into the garden to control these pests.

Gooseberry bushes can grow for as long as twenty years or more, and each plant produces three to four pints of berries per season. Added up, that's a lot of gooseberries for any one gardener to enjoy. Share them with neighbors and friends, or go ahead and keep them all for yourself. Either way, gooseberries are one fruit you'll not soon forget.

Gooseberry Chutney

FRESH GOOSEBERRIES ARE difficult to find and are only available during the summer months, but some specialty grocers carry them. When choosing fresh gooseberries, select firm, fresh berries of uniform color. Before using, "top and tail" them—that is, cut off the small stems and tops—with kitchen shears. If fresh gooseberries are not available, canned or frozen may be substituted.

3 pounds gooseberries
1 large onion, finely chopped
1 cup water
1 pound sugar
2 teaspoons salt
1 tablespoon ground ginger
⅓ teaspoon cayenne pepper
2 cups vinegar

Top and tail the berries and roughly chop them. In a large pot, cook the onion and gooseberries in water until well softened. Add all other ingredients and simmer, stirring occasionally, until the chutney thickens. Bottle while hot and cover immediately. The flavor of this chutney will mellow the longer it is kept.

YIELD: 4–5 cups

CHARLOTTE BRONTË

Ivy Recesses

TALK OF IVY recalls the climbing vines that cover English country homes or the bucolic settings of eastern colleges. But the lavish use of ivy on buildings is only one way to take advantage of this amazing plant. Ivy can creep up garden walls and trellises or provide ground cover in bare spots. Gardeners can shape ivy topiaries or, during the holidays, decorative living wreaths. With ivy, the garden can become a welcoming, shady retreat that remains green year-round.

Although ivy can appear delicate when first planted, it is hardy and becomes quite full when mature. Most varieties do well in shade, so they can be used to cover the exposed base of a bush or a garden nook that doesn't receive much sun. English ivy is the most popular type for landscapes and buildings. Vigorous and fast-growing, it can be trained to cover just about anything. Baltic ivy is another hardy outdoor variety suitable for most climates. Dentata is a rapidly growing, tough ivy that can easily scale a tall wall or trellis.

When choosing ivy, select a healthy plant suited to the outdoors; many ivies commonly sold in pots will only survive as indoor plants. Plant in a hole slightly larger than the plant's root ball. With the neck of the plant at soil surface, gently spread its roots across the ground. Place soil firmly around the roots. If planting for wall cover, place as close to the wall as possible and tie the ivy loosely to wall nails to guide it. Ivy loves moisture, so water well when the soil is dry until the plant is established. Prune the ivy each spring to maintain its size and shape if needed.

Ivy can also be trained around forms of wire to create whimsical designs. Make a living wreath by shaping a length of aluminum wire into a circle. Then bend the ends of the wire outward and anchor it into a pot full of soil. Plant young ivies at the base of each end of wire and tie their stems loosely to the form until they grow to meet at the top of the ring. These wire forms can be placed on a table or against a wall for a stunning effect. And an arched, ivy-covered trellis always makes a dramatic entryway.

Through the Looking-Glass

"It's no use talking about it," Alice said, looking up at the house and pretending it was arguing with her. "I'm *not* going in again yet. I know I should have to get through the looking glass again—back into the old room—and there'd be an end of all my adventures!"

So, resolutely turning her back upon the house, she set out once more down the path, determined to keep straight on till she got to the hill. For a few minutes all went on well, and she was just saying "I really *shall* do it this time—" when the path gave a sudden twist and shook itself (as she described it afterwards), and the next moment she found herself actually walking in at the door.

"Oh, it's too bad!" she cried. "I never saw such a house for getting in the way! Never!"

However, there was the hill full in sight, so there was nothing to be done but start again. This time she came upon a large flower-bed, with a border of daisies, and a willow-tree growing in the middle.

"O Tiger-Lily!" said Alice, addressing herself to one that was waving gracefully about in the wind, "I *wish* you could talk!"

"We *can* talk!" said the Tiger-Lily, "when there's anybody worth talking to."

Alice was so astonished that she couldn't speak for a minute: it quite seemed to take her breath away. At length, as the Tiger-Lily only went on waving about, she spoke again, in a timid voice—almost in a whisper. "And can *all* the flowers talk?"

"As well as *you* can," said the Tiger-Lily. "And a great deal louder."

"It isn't manners for us to begin, you know," said the Rose, "and I really was wondering when you'd speak! Said I to myself, 'Her face has got *some* sense in it, though it's not a clever one!' Still, you're the right colour, and that goes a long way."

"I don't care about the colour," the Tiger-Lily remarked. "If only her petals curled up a little more, she'd be all right."

Alice didn't like being criticized, so she began asking questions. "Aren't you sometimes frightened at being planted out here, with nobody to take care of you?"

"There's the tree in the middle," said the Rose. "What else is it good for?"

"But what could it do, if any danger came?" Alice asked.

"It could bark," said the Rose.

"It says 'Bough-wough!'" cried a Daisy. "That's why its branches are called boughs!"

"Didn't you know *that*?" cried another Daisy. And here they all began shouting together, till the air seemed quite full of shrill voices. "Silence, every one of you!" cried the Tiger-Lily, waving itself passionately from side to side, and trembling with excitement. "They know I can't get at them!" it panted, bending its quivering head towards Alice, "or they wouldn't dare to do it!"

"Never mind!" Alice said in a soothing tone, and, stooping down to the daisies, who were just beginning again, she whispered, "If you don't hold your tongues, I'll pick you!"

There was silence in a moment, and several of the pink daisies turned white.

"That's right!" said the Tiger-Lily. "The daisies are worst of all. When one speaks, they all begin together, and it's enough to make one wither to hear the way they go on!"

"How is it you can all talk so nicely?" Alice said, hoping to get it into a better temper by a compliment. "I've been in many gardens before, but none of the flowers could talk."

"Put your hand down, and feel the ground," said the Tiger-Lily. "Then you'll know why."

Alice did so. "It's very hard," she said; "but I don't see what that has to do with it."

"In most gardens," the Tiger-Lily said, "they make the beds too soft—so the flowers are always asleep."

This sounded a very good reason, and Alice was quite pleased to know it. "I never thought of that before!" she said.

"It's *my* opinion that you never think *at all*," the Rose said, in a rather severe tone.

"I never saw anybody that looked stupider," a Violet said, so suddenly, that Alice quite jumped; for it hadn't spoken before.

"Hold *your* tongue!" cried the Tiger-Lily. "As if *you* ever saw anybody! You keep your head under the leaves, and snore away there, till you know no more what's going on in the world, than if you were a bud!"

"Are there any more people in the garden besides me?" Alice said, not choosing to notice the Rose's last remark.

"There's one other flower in the garden that can move about like you," said the Rose. "I wonder how you do it—" ("You're always wondering," said the Tiger-Lily), "but she's more bushy than you are."

"Is she like me?" Alice asked eagerly, for the thought crossed her mind, "There's another little girl in the garden, somewhere!"

"Well, she has the same awkward shape as you," the Rose said: "but she's redder—and her petals are shorter, I think."

"They're done up close, like a dahlia," said the Tiger-Lily: "not tumbled about, like yours."

"But that's not your fault," the Rose added kindly. "You're beginning to fade, you know—and then one can't help one's petals getting a little untidy."

The Garden of Live Flowers

TO CREATE YOUR own garden of live flowers, consider flowers that bloomed in the yard of your childhood home, fragrant blossoms that recall special occasions, or the brightly colored blooms that have always tempted you from flower shop windows. In other words, plant a collection of personal favorites that speak to you.

Violets are a cheery, old-fashioned choice, and they're easy to grow. Sow their seeds in early spring to see blooms the following fall. Violet seeds can also be sown in late summer. If possible, transplant the seedlings to a cold frame or greenhouse for winter protection. The seedlings can be returned to the garden in early spring as soon as the ground can be worked.

Violets are hardy from Zones 3 to 5 and grow from four to six inches high. Colorful flowers bloom in blue, purple, pink, and white. Violets prefer full sun to partial shade. Set the seedlings ten to twelve inches apart in well-drained garden soil that has been enriched with additional leaf mold, well-rotted manure, or peat. Pests and disease are not usually a problem. The plants can be divided after flowering or in the fall to maintain the health of the plant and increase the supply of violets. Violets are especially useful as a ground cover under shrubs and trees. They also complement bulbs, wildflowers, and perennials.

The dwarf daisy is another favorite. Also known as the English daisy or *Bellis perennis*, this flower is hardy to Zone 3. A delicate spring bloomer, it grows as high as eight inches and is a generous self-sower. It prefers partial shade and struggles in long, hot summers. To grow, sow seeds in late summer or early autumn in protected areas or cold frames. Transplant the seedlings to flower beds in the spring, as soon as the ground can be worked. Place plants five inches apart.

Another popular choice is the easy-care Shasta daisy, which produces three- to four-inch white-petaled blossoms with yellow centers. The plant grows two to three feet high and will brighten any space in the garden or in pots on a patio. A happy summertime bloomer and great cutting flower, it thrives in a partially to totally sunny spot. Hardy from Zones 3 to 10, the Shasta daisy can also be grown in seaside locales.

LEWIS CARROLL

In early spring sow seeds in rich, well-drained soil. Seedlings are also available and should be set out in early spring, twelve inches apart. Spread mulch around the base of the plants to retain moisture, maintain consistent soil temperature, and add an attractive finishing touch. Daisies will clump together and should be divided every other spring. To do this, simply split the clump apart with a garden pitchfork and replant. Division will keep the plants healthy and productive. An added plus: There aren't any serious pests or diseases to contend with, but do keep an eye out for aphids. Snip off the flowers as they begin to fade, a process called deadheading. This simple procedure will promote a healthy plant and continued bloom. Common varieties include Alaska, Little Miss Muffet, and Polaris.

Shasta's cousins, the painted daisies, are bold and brilliant. Their feathery green foliage is a lovely complement to their colorful white, pink, and red blossoms. The spindly stems may require support. This plant produces flowers from June through July, grows from fourteen to twenty-four inches high, and is hardy to Zone 4. Painted daisies will enliven any landscape and are especially delightful when displayed in terracotta pots on windowsills.

Sow seeds indoors six to eight weeks before spring's last frost to get a jump start in the garden, or directly into the garden after the last frost. To prepare the garden soil, mix in compost, leaf mold, or well-rotted manure. Place seedlings twelve inches apart in a sunny spot in rich, damp soil.

KEY

DAISIES:
DWARF SHASTA
PAINTED
TIGER FLOWER
TIGER LILY
FOXGLOVE (YELLOW)
NEPETA MUSSINII (BLUE)
YARROW (YELLOW)
CARPATHIAN HAREBELL (BLUE)

Keep watered until the plant is established or doesn't show signs of wilting. Cut the plant back after the last bloom to encourage repeated blossoming. Like the Shastas, these daisies will clump up and need to be divided in late summer every three years. Simply lift the clump with a garden pitchfork, divide, and replant.

The oxeye daisy is a common roadside flower known for its two-inch white petals and yellow centers. It can also be cultivated in the garden, where its crisp, pure-white flowers will bloom throughout summer.

To add splashes of color to beds and borders or to fill in empty spaces, plant oxeyes in pots that can be toted about the garden. This cheerful daisy is hardy from Zones 2 through 10.

May Queen is an oxeye variety known for its long blooming season. Sow seeds or set out plants after the last frost in average garden soil. Choose a site that receives partial to full sun. If properly cultivated, oxeyes will grow from one to three feet high and spread up to two feet wide. Pests and diseases are minimal.

For a contrasting look, try the striking delphinium. Hardy in Zone 7 and southward as an annual, and for Zones 4 to 6 as a perennial, this luscious flower blooms in June and occasionally again in the fall. Tall spikes—up to eight feet—are lined with flowers of white, blue, yellow, pink, and lavender. Plant sturdy nursery plants in a sunny position in the spring. Delphiniums are heavy feeders and require a soil rich in nutrients. Before planting, cover the planting area with a two-inch coat of seasoned manure, compost, or a mix of the two. Mix these additives into the soil to a depth of six to eight inches. Spread a layer of 5-10-5 fertilizer on top of that and then another two-inch layer of compost and manure. Mix thoroughly and water deeply. Plant delphiniums two feet apart. The crown of the plant should be at soil level. A garden stake should be inserted with each plant; it is better to put the stakes in right away so the roots won't be harmed. Water regularly until established, and in drought conditions.

After the delphinium has completed blooming, cut the stalk just below the lowest bloom and prune after new leaves emerge to give the flower a nice shape.

Mix manure and compost into the soil again in the fall. Delphiniums are susceptible to slugs and powdery mildew. Use traps to lure slugs away. To treat powdery mildew, a fluffy white coating that appears on the leaves, dust the infected area with sulfur. For further insurance, plant disease-resistant and pest-resistant cultivars.

A majestic stand of foxglove (or *digitalis*) is also a longtime favorite for the flower garden. These towering beauties are laden with two- to three-inch bell-shaped flowers of pink, rose, and purple, with dark spotted centers. Foxgloves are hardy from Zones 3 to 8 and grow up to five feet tall. They flower throughout summer and will rebloom if pruned back after the first flowering.

Plant foxgloves in spring or fall near the center or at the back of the garden, in a mass along walls or fences, or mixed with other flowering shrubs. Select a moist but well-drained, humus-rich spot in full sun to partial shade. Seeds should be sown outdoors in the fall. New growth will emerge the following spring and will flower in the second growth year.

Foxgloves will self-sow if the stalks are left in place after flowering. There are no serious pests to worry about. However, overgrown clumps should be divided in spring or fall and replanted in soil enriched with organic matter, such as compost or manure. This will keep the plants healthy.

Another fine choice for your garden of live flowers is yarrow, a fibrous-rooted, aromatic herb that produces yellow, flat-topped flower heads in dense clusters four to five inches across. The flowers open in summer and last for several weeks. The flower heads can be dried for use in arrangements by wrapping four or five stems together and hanging them upside down.

Hardy in Zones 3 to 9, yarrow is a heavy spreader and grows three to four feet high and three feet wide in tight clumps. Plant in average, well-drained soil in full sun or light shade. Because of its heavy growth habit, plant yarrow at least four feet apart in the middle or back of the garden. To propagate, divide yarrow in early spring or fall and replant the healthier divisions into soil treated with organic matter, or take tip cuttings in spring or early summer, dip into rooting hormone (available in most nurseries), and replant in soilless mix. After roots have developed, the seedlings can be planted in the garden.

Yarrow is susceptible to powdery mildew. To eliminate, remove the affected parts of the plant and dust the healthy plant with sulfur.

Whatever mix of talkative flowers you grow, keep in mind how they will share their home. Plant tall flowers in back so they don't shade their shorter, sun-loving neighbors. When the flowers are happy, their contentment will be contagious.

The Shrill Little Daisies

THE ENGLISH DAISY, *Bellis perennis*, is a charming little flower often used to edge pathways or provide a bright spot of color at the front of a perennial border in spring. It can be followed by lobelia or sweet alyssum in summer for a pleasing effect. English daisies provide an excellent contrast to taller plants, such as perennial phlox and sweet William, and they look lovely mixed in with fruit trees and roses. The mix of height and color adds an element of interest to the garden.

The six-inch-high stems grow in small clumps of dark green leaves and produce dense needlelike petals in single or double strains. The red, pink, and white flowers are one to two inches across and are punctuated with bright yellow centers. Long ago, the plants were known as "day's eye" because of this yellow eye. The plants begin to flower in June and will continue through early July. In cool coastal areas of California, the plants will blossom all year.

New plants can be started from seeds sown in the garden in spring or summer, but they won't flower until the following spring. Mature plants should be treated as annuals. Set plants out in mid-April eight to nine inches apart in a rich, moist soil amended with manure or compost. Daisies thrive in full sun but will tolerate light shade. Water with a liquid fertilizer and add a blanket of mulch to maintain moisture and prevent weeds.

Aphids are the greatest threat to a healthy plant and often appear when the weather begins to warm. Evidence of their presence includes sticky, blistered, or blackened leaves. To control aphids, spray or use biological controls.

English daisies make excellent cut flowers and are easy—and enjoyable—to gather.

LEWIS CARROLL

❧ *Passionate Tiger Lilies* ❧

THE TIGER LILY, originally from China, lends an easygoing, old-fashioned elegance to the garden. It is a good choice for mixed borders and heirloom gardens. *Lilium lancifolium*, as it is known botanically, is distinguished by its dark purple spots and bold, salmon-orange color. Tiger lily hybrids, which are also spotted, are available in red, yellow, and white blooms.

Readily available at garden centers, tiger lily bulbs grow easily in Zone 4—and in containers—into plants that bloom in midsummer. Numerous grand flowers droop from four- to six-foot-tall stems from July into September, brightening the fall garden.

Plant bulbs deeply—at least seven inches down—in a light, loamy soil in the fall. As the ground warms, the bulb will begin to grow and store energy. During flowering, the storage organs are emptied of food. The foliage, however, will continue to grow after flowering, storing up food reserves for the next growing season. So don't cut back the foliage until it has begun to wither. If withering foliage is unsightly, plant other annuals to hide it.

The lily bulbs will multiply quickly and should be divided and replanted every three years. Propagation is done by division or by planting the black bulbils produced in the axils of the leaves.

Tiger lilies are generally untroubled by pests, unless the newly introduced red lily beetle is a problem in your area—in which case spraying is required (Neem, a botanical spray, mixed with a natural pyrethrum extract seems to work very well). Tiger lilies can also sometimes harbor a mosaic virus that can harm other lily species while leaving the tiger lilies untouched. If this turns out to be a problem in your garden, simply grow the lovely tiger lilies in an area away from its cousins.

Death Comes for the Archbishop

Once when he was riding out to visit the Tesuque mission, he had followed a stream and come upon this spot, where he found a little Mexican house and a garden shaded by an apricot tree of such great size as he had never seen before. It had two trunks, each of them thicker than a man's body, and though evidently very old, it was full of fruit. The apricots were large, beautifully coloured, and of superb flavour. Since this tree grew against the hillside, the Archbishop concluded that the exposure must be excellent for fruit. He surmised that the heat of the sun, reflected from the rocky hill-slope up into the tree, gave the fruit an even temperature, warmth from two sides, such as brings the wall peaches to perfection in France.

The old Mexican who lived there said the tree must be two hundred years old; it had been just like this when his grandfather was a boy, and had always borne luscious apricots like these.

🍃 An Apricot Tart 🍃

ORIGINALLY FROM CHINA, apricots have been around for more than 2,000 years. Apricots are delicate and bruise easily; in the grocery store, they are bedded individually in a box to keep them at their peak. Handle them carefully and look for fruit that has a smooth skin, gives slightly to the touch, and is free of blemishes. If they are immature, they can be ripened in a closed paper bag. Apricots may be refrigerated for up to a week. The skin of the apricot is thin and tender, so they are wonderful to eat out of hand. If desired, remove the skin by blanching them in water for thirty seconds to make peeling easier. After peeling, just cut them in half lengthwise, twist the halves apart to take out the pit, and enjoy the delectable essence of the apricot.

1 basic 9-inch single pastry dough

1 teaspoon flour

¼ cup apricot jam or preserves

¾ cup toasted slivered almonds, finely chopped

8 apricots, peeled, pitted, and halved

⅓ cup sugar

1 tablespoon unsalted butter, cut into small pieces

Preheat oven to 450°F. Place crust in 9-inch tart or pie pan. Spread flour over crust and pierce all over with a fork. Bake crust about 10 minutes, or until golden brown. Remove from oven, and reduce oven to 375°F. Spread jam or preserves over the bottom of the crust and sprinkle with the toasted almonds. Place apricots, cut side down, over almonds, filling crust completely. Sprinkle sugar over the apricots, dot with butter, and bake about 1 hour, until apricots are tender and the filling is syrupy. Cool on a rack before serving.

YIELD: 8 servings

Father Latour's recreation was his garden. He grew such fruit as was hardly to be found even in the old orchards of California; cherries and apricots, apples and quinces, and the peerless pears of France—even the most delicate varieties. He urged the new priests to plant fruit trees wherever they went, and to encourage the Mexicans to add fruit to their starchy diet. Wherever there was a French priest, there should be a garden of fruit trees and vegetables and flowers. He often quoted to his students that passage from their fellow Auvergnat, Pascal: that Man was lost and saved in a garden.

He domesticated and developed the native wild flowers. He had one hill-side solidly clad with that low-growing purple verbena which mats over the hills of New Mexico. It was like a great violet velvet mantle thrown down in the sun; all the shades that the dryers and weavers of Italy and France strove for through centuries, the violet that is full of rose colour and is yet not lavender; the blue that becomes almost pink and then retreats again into sea-dark purple—the true episcopal colour and countless variations of it.

A Blanket of Purple Verbena

VERBENA IS A low-maintenance, tender perennial often treated as an annual. Widely regarded for its adaptability, verbena thrives in cool weather, yet it's a dependable bloomer in hot climates. Garden verbena can be grown from Zones 3 to 10.

The bushy plants grow six to twelve inches high and produce clusters of small, starry flowers among dark green, spiked foliage. Verbena is an excellent selection for window boxes; it's one of the few flowers that can be counted on to bloom all summer long. Varieties produce purple, red, pink, white, or burgundy blossoms.

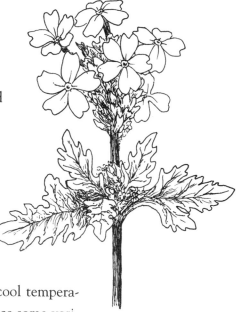

Verbena creates a sweeping profusion of color when planted in a mass along walkways and borders. It's also attractive interspersed throughout rock gardens. Different varieties make a bold statement when planted together in containers.

A limited selection of seedlings is available in garden centers in the spring. A much larger variety of seed true to color and form is accessible through garden catalogs. Sow seeds in late winter indoors and transplant in May after a two-week hardening off period; or simply transplant mature plants.

This cheery, drought-tolerant bloomer prefers a sunny, dry, and cool setting. The ideal site offers full sun, sandy soil, and cool temperatures. Plant eight to ten inches apart in containers and beds, since some varieties spread as much as twelve to eighteen inches across.

Verbena grows in mounded clusters. Small flowers bloom continuously from midsummer until fall. The flowers' beauty is highlighted when planted near the taller salvia, hollyhocks, foxglove, and delphinium.

The Garden Palette

IMAGINE A PAINTER'S palette, with its set of basic colors ready to be used alone or mixed to create different effects. The artist decides how to apply the paint to the canvas to bring to life the vision in his mind.

Gardeners perform a similar process. The garden space is the canvas and the plants and flowers the colors on the palette. The gardener's imagination brings them together in a way that satisfies a personal vision.

There are no set rules about combining flowers, plants, and trees. The gardener's individual preferences are the driving force behind any colorful garden scheme. But there are several realities to be considered in planning the garden. First, remember that the garden is an ever-changing landscape. As seasons change and years pass, the garden looks different every day; some flowers bloom and others die off. Consider how the colors of the plantings will change throughout the year. It's also advisable to use different kinds of plantings to vary the look of the garden. And plant trees, shrubs, vines, and flowers that blossom at different times throughout the season to provide continuous color. Keep in mind that the foliage of shrubs and trees can provide color even when they're not in bloom.

Choosing the colors to use in the garden can be tough. Should the flowers be all one color, or is a mix more attractive? Once again, it's personal preference. If a unicolor scheme is desired, try choosing a variety of shades. And don't discount the foliage, which brings its own color to the garden. Bright colors combine nicely with muted tones, such as creamy white among fiery red. Silver-toned plants provide a pleasing frame for more richly colored plantings.

Above all, be realistic. Use what's available and grows well in the area. Take into consideration the amount of time available for gardening, and plant what is manageable. Many gardens pictured in books or magazines have been years in the making and are continually monitored. Home gardeners may not have the luxury of shifting and replanting frequently to maintain the color scheme. Likely, some mistakes will be made along the way. But keep the faith—gardens that are alive with color are the incarnation of a gardener's dream.

WILLA CATHER

The Placement of Fruit Trees

GROWING FRUIT TREES is an easy and healthy way to add variety to the garden, and virtually any garden can accommodate some type of fruit tree. Just make sure to address these three main considerations: climate and soil, available space, and what type to grow.

The first step is figuring out which fruit trees will thrive in your climate zone. For example, a lemon tree planted outdoors in New England isn't hardy enough to survive the cold winter. Certain varieties of fruits are also zone-specific, so be sure to check with nursery professionals when choosing plantings.

Space isn't as limiting a factor in growing fruit trees as one might think. Even a small backyard patio can be home to potted dwarf trees if they're positioned well. But making the most out of any space requires planning. Before buying, take stock of the area you plan to use and note the sunlight available. Fruit trees all have one thing in common: They need full sunlight for best results. That means *at least* six hours of direct sun per day during the growing season (usually spring to late fall). Never place fruit trees where a building or larger tree shades them.

Be realistic: Plan enough space between the trees before planting. Whether your project's an apple orchard or a few plum trees in the backyard, the trees require ample growing room. Carefully consider the mature size of each when planning the space, and never disregard planting instructions regarding spacing. You'll be sorry you did—overcrowding fruit trees robs them of sunlight, water, and essential nutrients that prevent them from bearing healthy fruit.

What types of fruit trees to plant is a personal decision. Many gardeners prefer a mix of trees in the yard, like plums, apples, pears, cherries, and peaches. Consider how much fruit the trees will produce and how you'll use it so you don't end up wasting the bounty.

Fruit trees enjoy deep, well-drained soil. Fertilization and soil enhancements should be applied according to the individual needs of the type of fruit tree.

It's also important to ask at the nursery whether the trees are self-pollinating or if they require cross-pollination. If self-pollinating, only one tree of the type is required for fruiting. If cross-pollinating, two or more types of the tree are needed to insure fruiting. Also, beginners will do well with varieties of fruit trees that don't require a lot of maintenance such as pruning or spraying.

With a little planning, any gardener can find space for a fruit tree. Whether it's a healthy apple a day or cherries to top a decadent cheesecake, fresh fruit from the garden is a joy not to be missed.

 *Scents of Home*

POTPOURRI IS A popular, easy way to enjoy the colors and scents of the garden indoors without continually tending to fresh flowers. This blend of dried flowers, herbs, and spices adds fragrance to any room. Making potpourri is simple. All you need is some equipment that's probably already around the kitchen, readily available ingredients, and a colorful imagination.

To start, take out a large glass or glazed ceramic bowl for mixing. Plastic or wooden bowls used for food are not recommended, as they will absorb the smell of the potpourri. Next, locate a kitchen scale to measure ingredients, a mortar and pestle for crushing herbs and spices, and at least one eyedropper for adding the essential oils. Finally, have ready a large plastic bag or a paper bag lined with waxed paper—you'll need this to cure the potpourri.

Potpourri ingredients vary widely according to individual preference, but there are some basic elements. Dried flowers provide fragrance and color; herbs and spices add aroma; a fixative preserves the scent; and essential oil accentuates the fragrance.

The flowers can be harvested from the garden or bought at the store. Some common fragrant blooms include lavender, rose, jasmine, and lilac. Popular dried flowers that add color are cornflower, marigold, nasturtium, and periwinkle. Dried herbs and spices will provide an even more pungent fragrance. Lemon verbena, rosemary, cinnamon, cloves, and nutmeg are common choices, but the selection is limited only by your imagination. These can be home-dried or purchased whole, crushed, or powdered. The supermarket produce section often offers inexpensive refill bags of herbs and spices.

The ingredient that keeps the potpourri aromatic is the fixative. Orrisroot, benzoin, and storax help preserve the scent and are usually available in health food stores. The main scent of the potpourri comes from the essential oil, which is the pure oil of a flower, spice, or herb. The essential oil, available at specialty shops, provides a background for the other fragrant ingredients.

Assembling the potpourri is easy, but keep in mind this basic rule: All the ingredients—except the essential oils—should be completely dry. If the dried ingredients contain any moisture at all, the mixture may mold.

Combine the dried flowers, herbs, and spices in the bowl. Sprinkle the essential oil over the mixture with an eyedropper. Stir the potpourri gently with a wooden spoon, or mix it carefully with your hands to prevent crushing the flower heads. Cure the potpourri for at least two weeks to allow the aromas to meld. To do this, store the mixture in the plastic bag. Then, stir the contents or gently shake the bag every couple of days to redistribute the ingredients. Finally, pour the potpourri into a decorative bowl, place it on a table, and enjoy the lasting scent and color of the season.

Lavender Potpourri

5 oz. lavender flowers

2 oz. cornflowers

1 oz. marigold

3 oz. whole cloves

1 oz. crushed cloves

1 oz. cinnamon stick, broken into 1-inch pieces

½ oz. powdered cinnamon

½ oz. powdered allspice

1 oz. powdered orrisroot

15 drops lavender oil

Sources

Aphrodisia
264 Bleeker St.
New York, NY 10014
(212) 989-6440

Cherchez
P.O. Box 550
Front St.
Millbrook, NY 12545
(914) 677-8215

Alone, I should never have found the garden—except, perhaps, for the big yellow pumpkins that lay unprotected by their withering vines—and I felt very little interest in it when I got there. I wanted to walk straight on through the red grass and over the edge of the world, which could not be very far away. The light air about me told me that the world ended here: only the ground and sun and sky were left, and if one went a little farther there would be only sun and sky, and one would float off into them, like the tawny hawks which sailed over our heads making slow shadows on the grass....

I sat down in the middle of the garden, where snakes could scarcely approach unseen, and leaned my back against a warm yellow pumpkin. There were some ground-cherry bushes growing along the furrows, full of fruit. I turned back the papery triangular sheaths that protected the berries and ate a few. All about me giant grasshoppers, twice as big as any I had seen, were doing acrobatic feats among the dried vines. The gophers scurried up and down the ploughed ground. There in the sheltered draw-bottom the wind did not blow very hard, but I could hear it singing its humming tune up on the level, and I could see the tall grasses wave. The earth was warm under me, and warm as I crumbled it through my fingers. Queer little red bugs came out and moved in slow squadrons around me. Their backs were polished vermilion, with black spots. I kept as still as I could. Nothing happened. I did not expect anything to happen. I was something that lay under the sun and felt it, like the pumpkins, and I did not want to be anything more. I was entirely happy. Perhaps we feel like that when we die and become a part of something entire, whether it is sun and air, or goodness and knowledge. At any rate, that is happiness; to be dissolved into something complete and great. When it comes to one, it comes as naturally as sleep.

THE SYMBOL OF the autumn harvest, the pumpkin is native to the Americas. Most varieties originated in Mexico and Central America and were used all over North America by the American Indians. Pumpkins come in many sizes and make tasty Thanksgiving pies, charming trick-or-treat jack-o'-lanterns, or simply look wonderfully festive nestled beside the front door. Best of all, it is possible to make room for a patch in your own backyard.

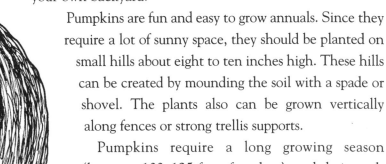

Pumpkins are fun and easy to grow annuals. Since they require a lot of sunny space, they should be planted on small hills about eight to ten inches high. These hills can be created by mounding the soil with a spade or shovel. The plants also can be grown vertically along fences or strong trellis supports.

Pumpkins require a long growing season (between 100–125 frost-free days), and their seeds need warm soil to germinate. Since each variety has its own germination schedule, it is important to consult the package to determine the proper sowing time. Seeds are available through local garden centers or mail-order catalogs. In general, the seeds can be sown directly in the garden in spring after the last frost, or started indoors two to three weeks before the last expected frost. If started indoors, great care must be taken not to disturb the roots in the transplanting process.

To plant, dig a hole two feet across and eighteen inches deep for each hill of pumpkins. The hills should be spaced six to ten feet apart, the farther the better. If the hills are closer than ten feet, it will become necessary to train and prune the vines. Add several shovelsful of compost and manure to the soil and fill the hole, mounding it higher in the center. Roots will thrive in the deep, rich soil, encouraging the plants to become productive.

Place six seeds in a circle on each hill, about four to six inches apart. Gently push each seed into the hill about an inch, cover with soil, and water. After most of the seeds have germinated, choose the two most healthy-looking seedlings and remove the others. If the seedlings aren't thinned, the plants will produce lovely foliage but no fruit.

The hills should be watered, weeded, and mulched until the plants begin to vine. After that, the leaves will cover the hills and prevent weed growth. As the pumpkins grow, keep the soil moist by watering the hills evenly. Feed weekly with a bucket of liquid fertilizer, such as Miracle-Gro, that will penetrate directly to the roots.

Common pests to watch for are the squash borers and cucumber beetles. Borers are a particular problem as they tunnel through the stems, causing entire sections of the plant to wilt. To prevent damage, you can use row covers made from lightweight plastic fabric. They can be stretched over hoops and anchored to the ground so they cover the plants, permitting water, light, and air to reach the plants, but keep out pests. Keep in mind, though, that the covers may need additional ventilation on sunny days. However, if pumpkins are grown in well-manured soil, borers are rarely a major concern, as the vines will root wherever they come in contact with the rich soil. These additional mini-root systems will allow the plants to resist most any damage the borer may cause.

Diseases such as wilts, leaf spot, and mildew are also common and can be prevented by crop rotation, fungicide applications, and good air circulation. It is always wise to check with the local county extension agent or garden center about problems specific to the area.

Pumpkins are ready for harvest when their skins have turned orange, their shells have hardened, or the vine has begun to wither. When harvesting, leave a three- to four-inch stem on the fruit; otherwise, rot will swiftly set in. Be sure to harvest before any heavy frost. Pumpkins can be stored in a cool, dry area (50° to 55° F) for several months.

Varieties to consider include Jack Be Little (a tiny, bright orange pumpkin good for decorating);

WILLA CATHER

71

Cheyenne Bush and Small Sugar (for pies); Connecticut Field and Cinderella (for jack-o'-lanterns); Snack 'R Jack (for edible seeds); Triple Treat (for edible seeds and jack-o'-lanterns); Spirit (a compact vine for small gardens); and Big Moon and Prizewinner (for pumpkins weighing as much as one hundred to two hundred pounds); Rouge Vif d'flampes (for pies and decoration).

So rest a tree stump amid the yellowing pumpkins for critter-watching, listening to the humming of the wind—or just taking a quiet break.

 *Pumpkin Pillows*

FRESH PUMPKINS ARE not hard to find, and they aren't hard to work with. Small sugar pumpkins are plentiful in the fall, and they are the best choice for cooking. Fresh pumpkins need to be peeled, seeded, and diced to make a proper puree for most recipes. Is this a daunting task? Not at all. Just cut the pumpkins in half, scoop out the seeds, then roast the halves on a greased baking sheet in a 450°F oven until they're soft—generally thirty-five to forty-five minutes. Throw the seeds on another greased baking sheet and roast those for eight to ten minutes for a snack while cooking. Once the pumpkin is roasted, the skin will come right off, and it's ready to be pureed.

Canned pumpkin can be substituted in any recipe calling for fresh pumpkin puree. Canned pumpkin is actually quite good; the manufacturers can the pumpkin at the height of its ripeness, so most of the work is done for you without a loss of flavor.

1 cup pumpkin puree

¼ cup Parmesan cheese

½ cup ricotta cheese

½ cup toasted bread crumbs or amaretti

¼ teaspoon each ground cinnamon, nutmeg, and cloves

1 tablespoon chopped fresh sage

Salt and pepper, to taste

Fresh pasta sheets (can be homemade or purchased at a pasta shop)

Mix all ingredients (except pasta) in a large bowl, combining well. Cut pasta sheets into three-inch rounds with a biscuit cutter. Brush entire surface of pasta round with water. Place a teaspoon of filling to one side of the pasta. Fold pasta over to form a half-moon. Press dough around the filling, pushing out excess air (the ravioli may burst when cooking if too much air is left inside). Seal edges of pasta with a fork or a crimped pastry cutter. Cook pasta in 4 quarts salted boiling water. The ravioli are done when they rise to the top. Remove and drain well. These ravioli are best served simply with sage butter and sprinkled with Parmesan cheese.

YIELD: 6 servings

The Garden of Autumn Glory

THE FLOWER GARDEN is a delight in spring and summer when colorful new blossoms appear, but the gardening season doesn't have to end there. There are many plants available at nurseries that will flower in the autumn after the summer blooms have disappeared, giving the garden exceptional color. These flowers last well into the fall, extending the life of the garden until the first frost.

The most well-known autumn garden flowers are the chrysanthemums. These plants come in a wide variety of types and colors. They can be grown from seeds or cuttings, or bought as potted plants. The fragrance of the flowers makes them popular for cutting and for using in dried flower arrangements.

The varieties of chrysanthemums are categorized by the flower heads. The pompom type has one-and-one-half- to two-inch blossoms and grows up to two feet tall, while button chrysanthemums produce tight blooms that are less than an inch across. Single-flowered chrysanthemums are daisylike, with only a single row of petals. Even more decorative varieties of chrysanthemums produce large blossoms extending two to four inches across. The colors of any of these types range from white and yellow to shades of pink and lavender to brilliant red and bronze.

If being grown from seeds, they should be sown in early spring. Chrysanthemums should be planted in full sun and spaced twelve to twenty-four inches apart. Enrich the soil with compost or cow manure, and provide plenty of water. To produce the best blossoms, pinch back the growing tips of the plants after three or four pairs of leaves have formed in early August. Plants will blossom the following year.

Another beautiful and decorative plant for any fall garden is the Chinese lantern, or winter cherry. The plants are not grown for their flowers but for the orange red seed coverings that hang from the plant like chinese lanterns. These papery seed coverings house a bland scarlet berry known as a winter cherry. These plants grow one to two feet tall, with the decorative lanterns lasting well into September. They should be planted in full sun or minimal shade about two feet apart. Plant Chinese lanterns in rich, moist, well-drained soil, and keep them well watered. Cut and left to dry, the lanterns make lovely additions to dry arrangements.

Aphids and spider mites are common pests. Keep a watchful eye and take action right away if they're detected, as aphids are prolific breeders.

Another late-summer bloomer is garden phlox. These plants produce clusters of sweetly scented flowers with disk-shaped petals. They come in white, pink, red, blue, and purple. The flower clusters grow twelve to fourteen inches tall and six to ten inches across. Varieties include 'Bright Eyes,' which have pale pink blossoms with red centers, 'Everest,' with white flowers and rose-colored centers, and 'Starfire,' which has deep red blooms, and 'Mt. Fuji,' with blooms of purest white. Garden phlox should be planted in full sun or light shade in moist soil. The upper eight inches of soil should be enriched with compost. Cut off dying blooms to prevent reseeding, as the new plants won't be true to color. Removing the old blossoms will also help encourage a second blooming. Water regularly in hot weather to deter spider mites, and look for mildew-resistant varieties if powdery mildew is a problem in your area.

Goldenrod is an often-overlooked wildflower that brings lovely yellow flowers to the autumn garden. These tall plants yield ten- to twelve-inch flower heads filled with many tiny blossoms.

Goldenmosa grows up to thirty inches with tiny golden flowers. Peter Pan has canary-yellow flowers and grows two to three feet tall. Golden Dwarf tops out at twelve inches. Goldenrod should be planted in full sun or very light shade, about eighteen inches apart. Goldenrod will grow in just about any soil. If grown from seed, plants won't bloom until the second year. Goldenrod destined for a dried arrangement should be cut just before the flowers open.

The autumn garden can be filled with as many beautiful and fragrant flowers as the spring garden. Extending the garden season to include these fall flowers and plants will keep the glorious colors in the yard—and the winter blues at bay—a little while longer.

 ## Ornamental Grasses

ORNAMENTAL GRASSES MAKE a marvelous addition to any garden or landscape. They can stand by themselves as a central attraction in a garden, be used in clusters as ground cover or a screen, or light up a bare spot under a tree. Ornamental grasses can be bought at nurseries and garden centers, or seeds can be ordered from the sources listed below. They are easy to grow, look lovely, and will add a new dimension to any yard.

Ornamental grasses can be specific to certain regions, so check the climate zone recommendations carefully before purchasing. There are many varieties for Zones 4 to 9. These include *Miscanthus sinensis 'Varietgatus,'* or Maiden Grass, which has broad leaves with creamy white stripes. Use this alone as an accent, or in clusters as a hedge or screen. The Blue Fescue (*Festuca glauca*) is a medium-sized grass that grows twelve to sixteen inches tall. Grown in full sun, its leaves become an intense blue-gray color. *Rhynchelytrum repens*, also known as Natal Grass, is at home in a hot, sunny position. It grows to about a foot tall, and its charm is in the ruby-red flower heads that bloom in the summer. Squirrel-tail (*Hordeum jubatum*) is a favorite ornamental grass. It grows easily in full sun and produces soft, feathery heads that resemble squirrel tails.

It is best to buy young plants from a nursery, as they will take only two to three years to reach maturity. Grasses grown from seed take five to seven years to become fully developed. When ordering from a nursery, ask for a spring delivery. Check the plant carefully to be sure it is well established in the container. The plant should not dislodge from the pot when pulled gently, and there should be a mass of roots peeking out the bottom.

For best results, plant ornamental grasses in the early spring. If growing from seeds, start them indoors five to seven weeks before planting. To plant, dig a hole with straight sides and a flat bottom, to one-and-one-half times the size of the root ball. Add peat moss or garden compost to the soil before filling in around the new plant. Leave a ring of soil around the plant to create a basin to catch water to keep the roots moist. Water thoroughly after planting and cover the area with peat moss or garden compost immediately to provide moisture.

Ornamental grasses are low-maintenance plants. They should, however, be kept watered during dry spells and continually weeded. In autumn, cut back the plants to within two inches of the soil to keep them free from pests and disease during the winter. Cutting back also helps provide room for new growth in spring.

Ornamental grasses are becoming increasingly popular with home gardeners who want to add a new element to landscape designs. Grass isn't just for lawns anymore.

Sources

The Bath Nursery
2432 Cleveland Massillion Rd.
Akron, OH 44333
(330) 659-2080
www.mytownohio.com/tbn

Virtual Seeds Co.
P.O. Box 684
Selma, OR 97538
www.virtualseeds.com

The front yard was enclosed by a thorny locust hedge, and at the gate grew two silvery, moth-like trees of the mimosa family. From here one looked down over cattle-yards, with their two long ponds, and over a wide stretch of stubble which they told me was a ryefield in summer.

At some distance behind the house were an ash grove and two orchards: a cherry orchard, with gooseberry and currant bushes between the rows, and an apple orchard, sheltered by a high hedge from the hot winds. The older children turned back when we reached the hedge, but Jan and Nina and Lucie crept through it by a hole known only to themselves and hid under the low-branching mulberry bushes.

As we walked through the apple orchard, grown up in tall bluegrass, Ántonia kept stopping to tell me about one tree and another. "I love them as if they were people," she said, rubbing her hand over the bark.

In the middle of the orchard we came upon a grape arbour, with seats built along the sides and a warped plank table....

We sat down and watched them [the children]. Ántonia leaned her elbows on the table. There was the deepest peace in that orchard. It was surrounded by a triple enclosure; the wire fence, then the hedge of thorny locusts, then the mulberry hedge which kept out the hot winds of summer and held fast to the protecting snows of winter. The hedges were so tall that we could see nothing but the blue sky above them, neither the barn roof nor the windmill. The afternoon sun poured down on us through the drying grape leaves. The orchard seemed full of sun, like a cup, and we could smell the ripe apples on the trees. The crabs hung on the branches as thick as beads on a string, purple-red, with a thin silvery glaze over them. Some hens and ducks had crept through the hedge and were pecking at the fallen apples.

The Orchard (or Love Them As If They Were People)

APPLE TREES ARE favorites of home fruit growers because of their ability to adapt to different soils and climates. With so many varieties to choose from, any backyard orchardist can make a go of a few apple trees. Here are some general rules about selection, planting, and care that apply to all apple trees.

Choosing the type of apple tree to grow is dependent on a few essential factors. First, take a good look at the area available in the yard for planting. How much space do you have for your backyard orchard? Be realistic about the space you have, the light you have, and the soil you have to work with. The area should be in full sunlight for at least six to eight hours a day, have well-drained soil, and enough space to grow the two or more trees required for pollination. Dwarf stock trees need a seven-foot circle of growing space, semidwarf varieties should have a twelve-foot circle, and standard-sized apple trees need at least a twenty-foot circle of space between trees. Take a sheet of paper and sketch your orchard plot to scale, then mark the trees' locations, taking care to account for proper spacing.

Once the growing area has been established, next is the choice of the variety of apple to grow. Pay particular attention to the climate zone in the area when choosing apple trees. Choosing a tree for the wrong climate zone will insure disaster. Choose disease-resistant varieties for best results. Decide how the apples are to be used, whether for eating fresh, cooking, or even cider, to help determine what type of variety to pick. Lastly, remember that the fruit is the reason for the trees, so only plant as much as can be used. A standard-sized apple tree can produce up to three hundred pounds of fruit a season, so be conservative in deciding how many trees to plant.

The actual planting of the new apple trees in the fall or very early spring is pretty standard for most varieties. The main thing to keep in mind is to dig a big enough hole to prevent crowding of the roots. For bare root stock, dig the hole and add compost or manure and peat moss to the good topsoil from the hole. Replace the enriched soil in the hole, high enough that the tree's previous soil line is even with the ground. Pour a bucketful of water into the hole, let it drain a bit, then fill in with remaining enriched soil to just about the top. Leave a slight depression in the soil to catch water. The tree should be pruned right after planting to balance the top with the roots. Cutting back to a single whip will

WILLA CATHER

79

allow the roots to grow without the tree toppling over under the weight of the branches. For balled or potted trees, there is no pruning required as the roots are firmly implanted into soil before planting.

The fruit will not appear for two or three years after the initial planting, but the attention paid to the trees in that time will make all the difference in the fruit yield. The trees should be mulched with straw, leaves, or wood chips to retain as much water as possible. Place the mulch two to three inches away from the trunk, and water regularly. Pruning should be done to keep the strongest branches growing that will eventually bear the fruit.

Fertilize according to instructions for the tree variety to give the roots plenty of nutrients to help establish them well into the ground.

As the trees begin flowering and producing fruit, there are steps that can be taken to keep them healthy. To avoid disease and pests, keep the trees and the areas around them clean. Pick up and destroy any fruit from the ground, dispose of all pruned branches, and rake up all dead leaves around the trees to prevent nesting areas for pests. Prune the trees to let in more sunlight and air circulation, which discourages bugs and disease. If pesticides must be used, never spray while the tree is in bloom to insure the pollinating bees will survive. Also, don't spray up to two weeks before harvest to keep the apples clean and safe for eating. A properly cared-for apple tree can produce fruit for up to thirty years.

Loving an apple tree as if it were a person makes perfect sense to the gardener's heart. What work a gardener puts into his apple trees, he'll get back and more in a bountiful harvest of delectable fruit.

Building the Frame for a Grape Arbor

THE ARBOR HAS long been used as a support for grapes and other climbing plants. The open woodworking lends itself quite nicely as a firm brace for clinging vines. It also provides ventilation and reduces the threat of disease by keeping ripening fruit off the ground. Moreover, elevated branches that are within easy reach are easier to prune. An arbor cloaked in luscious grapevines adds ornamental interest to the garden and creates a shady summer resting spot.

This simple structure brings both form and function to the garden setting—besides it's fun and easy to make. Only a handful of supplies is necessary. Materials include posts, beams, and rafters of pressure-treated lumber; water-repellent, noncorroding fasteners; galvanized nails and bolts; and rustproof screws.

Cedar and redwood, which naturally deter bugs and weather well, are good choices. Bamboo is another practical and economical option that is both sturdy and lasting. Bamboo poles should be at least one and one-half inches wide when used as structural supports and can be purchased in various lengths and widths through garden supply centers. Those in warmer climates may even have a convenient stand in the backyard in need of some harvesting. The posts should be made from four-by-fours, and the beams and rafters cut from two-by-fours or two-by-sixes. Above all, it is important to use properly sized lumber for a strong, durable structure.

A common design consists of six support posts, two cross beams, and five or six rafters. Sink the posts into the soil eighteen to thirty-six inches deep and ten feet apart. These posts become the main supports. They should be plumb on two sides, braced and set in concrete; allow at least twenty-four hours for the concrete to set. To create the roof of the structure, fasten two beams to the tops of the posts, and then the rafters to the tops of the beams. Connect the beams securely by notching or using fasteners. Extending the beams and rafters by twelve inches at the sides and ends will add to the decorative appeal.

When the arbor is complete and the cement has dried, fasten a stiff plastic netting around each post to train the grapevines to ramble over this new garden centerpiece. For more detailed instructions and additional design ideas, consult one of the numerous specialty books on garden structures found at most bookstores and in libraries.

❧ Training a Grapevine ❧

GRAPEVINES ARE PROLIFIC producers when established in a sunny, sheltered spot in well-enriched soil of high organic content. A softly graduating slope where water can drain and air can circulate makes an ideal location for these vining plants.

Grape plants can be found at garden centers, large home improvement stores, or through mail-order catalogs. Bare-root plants should be planted in early spring; container-grown vines may be planted at any time, providing the ground can be worked.

Varieties of grapes are distinguished by their color, taste, growing needs, and whether they're meant for the table or wine. Table grapes can be grown in cool and warm areas, though in cool areas they require a sunny, warm wall or greenhouse. These grapes are available in early-, mid-, or late-season varieties. Their fruit comes in colors of blue, white, red, black, and gold; seedless types are also available.

Wine grapes grow best in areas that enjoy long, dry, sunny summers. In cooler climates, early- and midseason varieties can be grown on warm walls. Wine grapes also come in varieties that bloom at different times throughout the season. Some types are seedless, and colors are white, gold, black, blue, red, and bronze.

In general, plan to plant in the spring, placing the vines eight to ten feet apart in holes twelve inches wide and twelve inches deep. If the grapes are being grown for wine, plant as many vines as space will allow. For each plant, prune all but a single cane and all but two buds on that cane. The canes must be pruned after fruiting to foster the growth of new shoots for the next year. Each year, the shoots that grow from last year's canes will produce new fruit. The new shoots should be trained to a support to keep the fruit off the ground and to allow for sunshine and air to filter in.

Table grapes should be pruned regularly so the vines produce fewer—but tastier—grapes. Wine grapes should be pruned with the goal of maximizing the harvest.

Since crops deplete nutrients from the soil, it should be enriched with a high-potassium fertilizer every two to three weeks. If growth is poor, use a fertilizer with a high level of nitrogen instead. Stop feeding as soon as the grapes begin to ripen.

Training grapevines is a time-consuming but worthy endeavor. Vine-training structures include pergolas, arches, and arbors that provide ventilation and easy access for pruning and harvesting. A number of vine-training methods exist to suit personal preference and space requirements. These include the single, double, or multiple cordon. One method commonly employed by grape growers is a simple wire trellis. It involves a series of posts set twenty-four inches apart and strung with two rows of wire, one thirty inches from the ground and another twenty-four to thirty inches from the first wire. This method can be effective for the novice growing grapes on a country slope or in a backyard. The goal is to train a four-armed, single-stemmed plant over a period of three years.

In the first two years, the single stem is trained against a post. Several buds are left in place to grow above the upper wire and a couple under the lower wire. All other buds and blossoms must be pruned. As the buds develop, the four strongest stems are secured to the wires to become the fruiting arms.

Prune back the fruiting arms to six to ten buds each. Other than two stubs at the base of each fruiting arm, all other lateral canes must be removed. It is important to keep the vines pruned each year to ensure fruit for the next.

The single-cordon method involves the complex development of a single main trunk and several branches grown laterally from the sides. The double- and multiple-cordon methods include the development of more than one main trunk. All buds and fruit are likewise eliminated the first two years, and the fruit is allowed to grow the third year.

The grower isn't the only one who will want to enjoy the fruit; be on the lookout for birds, as well as pests and their calling cards: scales (sooty and spotted leaves with moldy spots); black vine weevils (holes in the leaves); spider mites (pale and mottled leaves); white flies and/or aphids (a sticky substance on leaves); wasps (cavities in vines); mealy bugs (a fluffy white substance on leaves); and diseases such as downy mildew and gray mold. All these conditions can be remedied using a variety of insecticide sprays, and in the case of wasps and birds, plants can be covered with panty hose or muslin.

Whether you make your home in the country or the suburbs, a lane of neatly pruned grapevines will give that old-world quality to the garden and enrich the table with bountiful harvests.

WILLA CATHER

🍂 Mulberry Jam 🍂

MULBERRIES ARE SMALL trees (to 30') that produce a delicious fruit similar in size and shape to the blackberry. They were first commercially grown in the United States not for their fruit, but for their leaves—the favorite food of the silkworm. While the silk experiment didn't prove successful (nor did the commercial growing of the fruit, which doesn't ship well), mulberries did become established over much of the Eastern Seaboard and now can be found throughout the United States. There are three principal types: black, white and red. The fruit produced by these varieties corresponds more or less to their names, though fruit of the white variety can be confusingly white, pink or even purplish.

You can buy mulberry trees from specialty growers (they grow very quickly, often producing fruit in just a few years), or you can harvest fruit from trees in the wild. You may even sometimes find mulberries in a local produce market or a summer farmers' market, as some fruit growers have mulberry trees and harvest the berries for local sale. Fresh berries should be used immediately; they may also be frozen. The juice of the mulberries stains badly, so take precautions when picking or walking near a mulberry tree. A clean way to collect the berries is to set a cloth down under the tree and give it a good shake. The berries should fall off the tree and can be gathered up in the cloth.

1 quart stemmed mulberries, ¾ quart ripe and ¼ slightly underripe

3 cups sugar

¼ cup lime juice or cider vinegar

½ teaspoon ground cinnamon

Cover mulberries in cold, salted water. Let stand 5 minutes. Drain, then rinse in cold water 3 times. Crush berries, add sugar, lime juice or cider vinegar, and cinnamon. Cook slowly, stirring, until the sugar dissolves. Boil rapidly, stirring constantly to prevent scorching, until jellying point is reached. Remove from heat; skim. Ladle into hot, sterilized jars to within ⅛ inch of jar top. Wipe jar rim and adjust lids. Process in boiling water bath 5 minutes. Remove from water bath and complete seals.

YIELD: 1½ pints

❧ The Currant Bush ❧

CURRANT BUSHES ARE easy to grow and take up little room in the yard. They thrive best in cool, moist climates but can be grown just about anywhere in the United States except the hottest and driest areas. Buying a 1- to 2-year-old plant from a nursery will yield the best results. They should fruit the first year after planting.

There are three types of currants: black, red, and white. Black currant bushes are not readily available in the United States because they were thought to host blister rust that can kill white pines within a 900-foot area. The most common types of the currants are the red and white. Popular types of the red variety are Red Lake, Perfection, Cherry, and Red Cross. These bushes produce the bright red berries used in preserves and jellies. Popular white currant varieties are White Grape and the White Imperial. The white berries, which are cream-colored, and almost translucent, are used fresh in desserts. If the berries aren't destined for the dinner table, try ornamental currants; they produce lovely, large blooms, but the fruit is rather bland. These types include the Buffalo Currant, the Flowering Currant, and the Missouri Currant.

Currants should be planted in the late fall or early spring and can tolerate a site with some shade, though fruiting is better in full sun. Any soil that is good for planting flowers or vegetables will be fine as long as the soil is heavily enriched with manure or compost before planting. Allow 5 feet between bushes. Water the new plants well, and keep the soil moist by laying two inches of hay, straw, or leaves around the base.

Keep the bushes watered properly if the rainfall is less than an inch or so a week. Fertilizing isn't necessary the first year, but the bushes should be fertilized with manure or compost every year thereafter. Currants do best with natural fertilizers. The fruit should appear in the late summer and early fall. At the end of the season, the bushes should be pruned. Keep three or four of the healthiest shoots, and cut back the others to the base. Every year after, keep cutting away the weakest shoots for better fruit clusters or flowers on the ornamentals.

Currants reach their full fruiting potential at about five years, and they can bear fruit for up to thirty years. There have been reports of bushes fruiting well into their fortieth or fiftieth year. For making jams and preserves, the fruit should be colored but not fully ripe when picked. To eat right off the bush, let the berries hang for about three weeks before harvesting. Just twist off the clusters, pluck the berries from the stem, and enjoy your sweet crop.

CHARLES CHESTNUTT

The House Behind the Cedars

He walked slowly past the gate and peered through a narrow gap in the cedar hedge. The girl was moving along a sanded walk, toward a gray, unpainted house, with a steep roof, broken by dormer windows. The trace of timidity he had observed in her had given place to the more assured bearing of one who is upon his own ground. The garden walks were bordered by long rows of jonquils, pinks, and carnations, inclosing clumps of fragrant shrubs, lilies, and roses already in bloom. Toward the middle of the garden stood two fine magnolia-trees, with heavy, dark green, glistening leaves, while nearer the house two mighty elms shaded a wide piazza, at one end of which a honeysuckle vine, and at the other a Virginia creeper, running over a wooden lattice, furnished additional shade and seclusion. On dark or wintry days, the aspect of this garden must have been extremely sombre and depressing, and it might well have seemed a fit place to hide some guilty or disgraceful secret. But on the bright morning when Warwick stood looking through the cedars, it seemed, with its green frame and canopy and its bright carpet of flowers, an ideal retreat from the fierce sunshine and the sultry heat of the approaching summer.

The Garden Walk

WARWICK WAS SPYING on a girl in her garden. (That's not nice, but in literature, it's not unusual.) He observed that she was at home in her garden, making her way along the garden walk. This walk was bordered by a congregation of flowering creatures, all calling for the girl's attention.

Every successful border presents this dynamic: a collection of plants—think of it as a classroom filled with fidgety kindergarteners—each of which is trying to outdo the other to get your notice. They strain and reach and wave their arms; "Over here! Over here!" they seem to clamor. They use their color, size, shape, texture, and range to compete for your glance. This is not to say the loudest (or tallest or brightest) wins this contest, but you can appreciate how each uses its most distinguishing features to best effect.

The girl's border garden was composed of a cast of characters, each with its own job to do, each with its own gift. The delicate, sunny jonquils and the smiling pinks and carnations were the friendly greeters. These flowers were playing an important height and color role, to be sure, but they were also hiding the scuffed shoes and knobby knees of their seemingly grander neighbors, the shrubs and lilies and roses. As a group, these border mates weren't flashy or loud, but they were busy and purposeful—and probably doing everything they could to keep the roses from hogging the stage. This was not a loud or bloody battle for the girl's attention, perhaps, but it certainly was a thoughtful one.

If the flowers in your borders aren't fighting for your attention—if they're merely politely and neatly coexisting—you're not giving your garden enough of a challenge to live up to. One needn't incite a riot in the border garden (although that can be fun); you just need to encourage a little friendly competition. Bring some new faces to the scene. Try a shape or color that is out of your usual range. Overfill the border ever so slightly so the plants are gently elbowing one another for the spotlight. In short, don't plant a border that *can* be ignored, for nothing's worse than a garden full of wallflowers.

LARGER YARD PLANTINGS, such as trees and hedges, should be planned carefully with an eye toward the future. Before any ground is broken, there are a number of factors to be considered.

The first step toward a successful landscape is making a plan on paper. Sketch the existing yard, preferably as close to scale as possible. Mark any buildings, structures, boundaries, and trees and shrubs. Walk around the property, noting the views from different vantage points, and jot down which areas could stand some improvement. Check those same views from the house—from all floors—noting how things look from inside. For instance, one side of the property may have a direct view of a neighbor's unsightly garage. In that case, taller plantings that could create a barrier between the properties would be preferable.

Keep a log of how the sunlight moves across the yard to determine what plants would thrive where. Determine the soil type and drainage areas that would affect any new trees or bushes. Be sure to list any existing utilities, both above and below ground. And keep in mind any future plans for the yard, such as a patio or a pool; leave space on the sketch for these.

Equally important to good planning is choosing the right trees and shrubs. The plantings should be suitable to the local climate and soil conditions. Consult local nursery experts when considering large plantings. Plants should be chosen with their purpose in mind. For example, trees may provide shade or fruit; a bush may flower or simply be a good thick hedge. Find out the plant's growth rate and habits as well as its height and width at maturity. A flowering dogwood may look lovely on the lawn but not near a walkway where it will drop slippery petals. A thick bush may seem appropriate for a hedge—until you discover that it loses its lower branches as it matures. Be sure to find out how much maintenance the plantings will require. You may decide you simply don't have the time to cultivate that vegetable garden you had your heart set on.

Your research will also uncover any unpleasant characteristics the plants are prone to, such as pests and diseases, weak wood, or invasive root systems. When it is finally time to plant, be sure to follow the directions for spacing—nothing is worse than overcrowding plants.

CHARLES CHESTNUTT

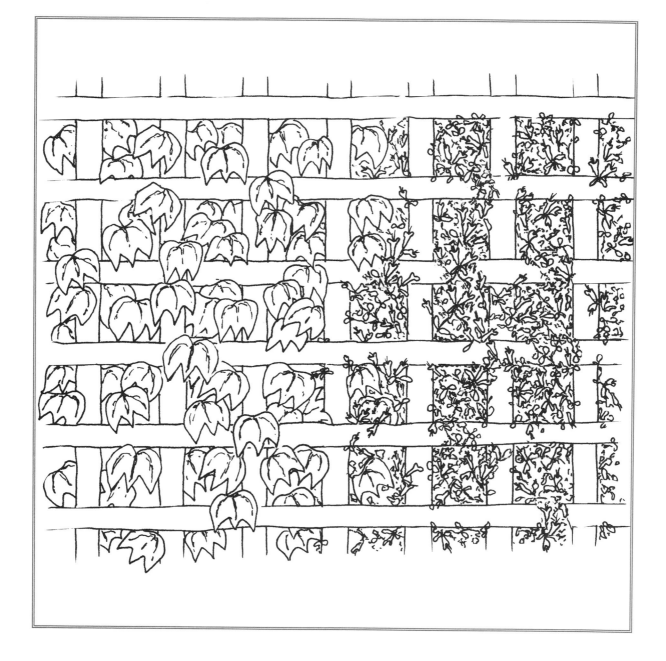

Whether it's a line of cedars down the driveway or a hedge of boxwood around the garden, a home landscape should be planned to make the most of the space. A good landscape design doesn't happen overnight, either as the plants grow, or as the landscape changes day to day and year to year. Taking the time to plan for future growth in the yard is a small chore compared with the delightful results a little forethought will bring.

The Living Fence

VINES CAN BE trained to create living fences that can form cozy spaces in the garden or cover up man-made structures that aren't particularly pretty to look at. Choosing the right vine for the job requires a few decisions and then doing a little research.

First, determine what role the vine needs to play. Is it for shading a sunny area, or does that chain-link fence around the pool need a disguise? A vine on a freestanding trellis can be used to hide the kids' toys or to separate one area of the garden from another. Second, since vines need to be trained on a support, check the availability of existing structures or whether you'll need to furnish one. For instance, a wisteria planted for shading a terrace will need an arbor or pergola built, but a black-eyed Susan vine used to cover a chain-link fence can be trained up the fence itself.

Next comes the decision about what kind of vine is appropriate to plant. Find out how fast the vine will grow. Annuals like sweet pea or morning glory can be expected to cover a space quickly for a single season, perhaps while a slower-growing perennial vine is being established. How large the vine will get is also important. A vine that grows to 30 feet at maturity needs considerable space and a very sturdy support to hold its weight and keep it upright through the seasons. Also, determine how the vine climbs. Some cling to flat surfaces with small holdfasts while others need to be able to twine around a support. Remember that vines that climb with holdfasts are generally not suited for wooden walls, which require periodic painting and maintenance.

CHARLES CHESTNUTT

Sun and shade are extremely important considerations and will limit your choices. Most vines need full sun, but luckily, there are some varieties like Virginia creeper and honeysuckle that can grow in partial shade. All vines need well-drained soil for best growth. If the soil in the selected area isn't very good, don't despair. The vines can be planted in tubs and trained up the support just as if they were planted in the ground. Finally, be sure the vine chosen will survive in the climate. A lovely bougainvillea that needs Southern warmth will never survive in the Northeast.

Vines and creepers occupy so little ground space that it's hard not to choose them to create natural draperies for your yard. They provide lovely flowers and foliage, but most of all, these living fences will provide a little privacy, plenty of distraction, and will blend naturally into any landscape. And if it's true that fences make good neighbors, the living fences you plant promise no end of neighborly goodwill.

Places

The tomato, fastened to stakes, will shine with a thousand globes, empurpled as June advances; see how many love-apples, violet aubergines and yellow pimentoes, grouped in an old-fashioned convex border, will enrich my kitchen garden…. There, garden, there! Don't forget you're going to feed me…. I want you decorative, but full of culinary graces. I want you flower-filled, but not with those delicate flowers bleached by a single cricket-chirping summer's day. I want you to be green, but not with the relentless greenery of palms and cacti, the desolation of Monaco, that simulated Africa. Let the arbutus glow beside the orange and the bougainvillaea's violet torches clothe my walls. And let mint, tarragon and sage grow at their feet, tall enough for the dangling hand to bruise their branches and release their urgent perfumes. Tarragon, sage, mint, savory, burnet—opening your pink flowers at noon, to close three hours later—truly I love you for yourselves—but I shan't fail to call on you for salads to go with boiled leg of mutton, to season sauces; I shall exploit you.

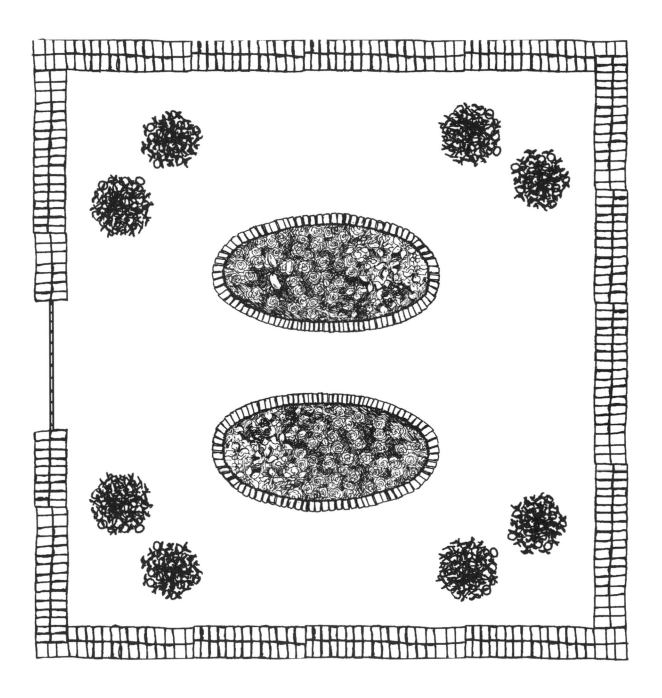

The Herb Garden That Begs to Be Touched

A CLUSTER OF herbs planted informally along a walkway enhances everyday comings and goings with its tempting fragrance. Pretty blossoms and leaves will beg to be touched, while a variety of textures and forms will add interest and charm. Herbs pull their own weight—they all have a use, be it in cooking, potpourri, home treatments, or simple decoration.

Throughout the years, herbs have been planted in formal and informal garden settings, often with a theme or particular use in mind or simply because they're nice to have around. A culinary garden can include an assortment of basil, oregano, thyme, rosemary, cilantro, mint, and tarragon for cooking, as well as others like parsley, borage, calendula and nasturtiums for garnishing. Shady areas make fine homes for sweet cicely, angelica, sweet violet, sweet flag, wild ginger, and sweet woodruff. Some herbs are more woody and grow as shrubs or trees. These include bayberry, herbal rose, rosemary willow, and sweet bay magnolia.

If space and time are at a premium, herbs can easily be integrated into the existing landscape, grown in containers, or kept on a sunny windowsill. They're hardy, easy to grow, and undemanding—and will sweetly reward the gardener with zesty flavorings for foods, pleasant scents for bedroom and bath, and splendid flowers for household arrangements.

A large variety of herbs, both annual and perennial, are available. There really is an herb for almost any location. Many herbs need sun, others shade. Some prefer dry soil and others a damp snuggery. Mix herbs together with flowers, vegetables, and shrubbery in sun or shade.

Planting an herb garden is easy. Most herbs are easily grown from seed; small starter plants are available as well. Most garden centers offer a fair variety of herbs in the spring and early summer. For rarer items, order from one of the many specialty herb nurseries around the country. Read the tag before planting to determine size at maturity. Dwarf varieties work well to keep the garden within bounds.

Be sure to check the plant's hardiness. Place small plants toward the front of the border and tall plants at the back or middle of an open garden so they won't shade the smaller plants. Herbs native to Mediterranean countries—including rosemary, catnip and lemon balm—need full sun and well-drained soil, and warm water temperature. If the winters are too cold in your area for a particular species, consider growing that variety in a pot, which you can sink into the ground during the summer and then take into a warm greenhouse or put on a windowsill for the winter.

Your chosen site should have good drainage and be fairly rich in organic matter. While herbs aren't fussy about soil, they do much better in well-prepared earth. This is particularly true of annual varieties, which will reward you with lush growth if you spend some time improving their soil with rotted manure or compost before planting.

Keep the plants well-watered until they are firmly established. During the growing season, herbs need at least one inch of water per week. Apply a one- to two-inch covering of mulch to retain moisture and discourage weeds.

Harvest often! Herbs can be used fresh or frozen, pressed, and dried. The more you pick, the more the plants will yield. When cutting, snip an entire piece of a stem; don't tear off individual leaves. And keep the blossoms pinched back—many herbs, like basil, won't be productive if they are allowed to flower and produce seed.

Culinary Graces: A Garden Herb Salad

SURPRISINGLY EARLY SPRING, even as an occasional snowflake falls to the earth, is a good time to take down the harvest basket and go foraging in the garden for an early crop of fresh salad herbs, such as sorrel, chives, arugula, watercress, or chervil.

Most delicately flavored summer herbs are splendid in a salad. They can be served alone or mixed with other lettuces. When selecting herbs for the salad, feel free to experiment and try new combinations. In general, very strongly flavored herbs, such as cilantro or sage, don't combine well with others, while more subtle herbs such as thyme or watercress, do.

In preparing a dressing, use a high quality olive oil. Its mellow texture will bring out the flavor of the herbs. Also try a mild white wine vinegar or, for an acidic flavor, wine vinegar mixed with lemon juice.

To harvest, carefully snip the tender leaves from the plants and remove small side leaves from the stem, which can be added to the compost bin. In a wooden bowl add a pressed clove of garlic, adjusted to taste. Add one tablespoon of salad or olive oil, one teaspoon herb vinegar, and salt and pepper to taste. Mix in the harvest of herbs. The herbs can also be marinated in an herb vinaigrette and served on a bed of lettuce.

Mix and match among spicy and mild, colorful and demure, or leaves and petals. The following herbs are tasty choices for a salad:

Anise (leaves)	Lovage (leaves)
Basil (leaves)	Marjoram (leaves)
Borage (leaves)	Mustard (young seedlings)
Burnet (leaves)	Nasturtium (leaves, petals)
Calendula (petals)	Oregano (leaves)
Chervil (leaves)	Parsley (leaves)
Chicory (leaves)	Rose (petals)
Chive (leaves, blossoms)	Savory (leaves)
Dill (leaves, umbrils)	Shallot (bulb)
Fennel (leaves, umbrils)	Sorrel (leaves)
Garlic (chives)	Sweet violet (petals)
Leek (leaves)	Tarragon (leaves)
Lemon balm (leaves)	Thyme (leaves)
Lime balm (leaves)	Watercress (leaves)

Herb Salad Vinaigrette

    1 cup olive oil
    ⅔ cup herbal vinegar
    1 clove garlic, minced
    ¼ teaspoon sugar
    ¼ teaspoon salt
    ⅛ teaspoon lemon balm

Mix ingredients in jar and shake again just before using. Dress salad sparingly so as not to overwhelm the flavors of the herb greens, then toss gently so as not to bruise leaves and petals.

Herb Vinegar

Simply put fresh herbs in a jar or bottle and cover completely with good quality red or white wine vinegar. Set the bottle aside for two to three weeks in the refrigerator to let the flavors blend. Strain, rebottle, and serve—or give as an elegant gift.

Heirloom Tomatoes

GROWING TOMATOES IS a tradition for many vegetable gardeners. They have their favorites and plant them year after year. But what many gardeners overlook are the old-fashioned varieties of tomatoes that taste like the ones their grandmothers served. Luckily, thanks to the efforts of seed savers across the country, these precious heirloom varieties are available once again. While modern tomatoes are more disease-resistant and uniform in size and color than their ancestors, they also tend to be less tasty. Heirloom varieties revive the tastes and colors of yesteryear, providing a spectacular flavor feast for today's gardener, unaccustomed to these poignant taste sensations.

The types and colors of heirloom tomatoes vary greatly. One of the most popular is Brandywine. This hearty, dark pink Amish variety fruits in mid- to late season. Big Rainbow is another favorite. Like Brandywine, this multicolored tomato requires a long season, so it may not be suited to areas with early frosts. (All tomatoes list days to maturity on the label—make sure that you have a sufficiently long season in your area to accommodate whatever varieties you choose.) Giant Belgium and Persimmon are also large, sweet varieties to investigate. Heirloom tomatoes are also available in medium- and small-fruited sizes, as well as cherry and pear types. Some heirlooms even come in surprising colors. Black Krim is a chocolate-colored tomato that will excite the eyes as well as the palate. Another wonder is White Beauty. This delicious, juicy, white-fleshed tomato will be a conversation-starter at any picnic.

Heirloom tomatoes can be grown like any other tomatoes, though you may have to start your own from seed, as they generally can't be found in most nurseries. Starting tomatoes from seeds is easy—simply plant the seeds in a pot or flat in a sunny window about 10 weeks before your last frost date. Be sure to leave your young plants outside, keeping them well-watered and in partial shade for a week or so before planting in the garden—they'll need that time to adjust to life outdoors. Heirlooms also require a lot more attention than modern hybrids—especially where pests are concerned. But give them plenty of sun and water, and they'll reward you with their secrets from the past. Keeping alive the tradition of heirloom tomatoes isn't difficult. The main challenge may come in deciding which of these beauties to grow in your garden.

❦ CHARLES DICKENS ❧

The Pickwick Papers

The rich, sweet smell of the hayricks rose to his chamber window; the hundred perfumes of the little flower-garden beneath scented the air around; the deep-green meadows shone in the morning dew that glistened on every leaf as it trembled in the gentle air; and the birds sang as if every sparkling drop were a fountain of inspiration to them. Mr. Pickwick fell into an enchanting and delicious reverie.

FLORAL SCENTS HAVE long been extracted, created, and combined to imitate the natural beauty of a fragrant garden. But growing your own aromatic garden is a pleasure that can't be duplicated.

Choosing the right plants—and the best placement for them—is not too difficult, as long as you keep a few guidelines in mind. Some modern varieties of formerly fragrant flowers may not be very scented. Often, new hybrids are bred to enhance bloom color and size, not smell. If possible, choose plants when they are in bloom, so you can get a sense of their individual fragrance. When choosing a site, select the warmest, most protected areas of the garden to produce the best results. Scents are more concentrated in warm, still air. A less windy location will ensure the fragrance will be savored in the air rather than dissipated by gusts of wind.

A key element in growing a scented garden is the placement of plants. In warm climates, a gardenia bush planted under a bedroom window will provide many sweet-smelling mornings. That same gardenia bush growing beneath a dining room window might be a nuisance; the strong smell of its flowers can interfere with the taste of food. Also keep in mind blooming times, and plan the garden to yield a sequence of flowering fragrance. For instance, lilacs start blooming in early May and fragrant peonies in June, while summer phlox finishes off the season in August and September. Unlike gardens planned for visual effect, don't cluster different plants that bloom at the same time. The fragrances may compete with each other, drowning out the individuality of each scent.

The fragrant garden begs the use of different types of plants. Flowers, bushes, trees, and herbs will round out the setting. Scented roses are an obvious choice, but try adding some hyacinth, narcissus, or carnations for variety. Common fragrant shrubs to try are the butterfly bush and summer-sweet. Mimosa and magnolia trees offer sweet, fruity scents that add another dimension to the garden. Easygoing herbs such as lavender, mint, and rosemary lend clean, fresh fragrances to the mix. For variety, add a couple of plants with fragrant foliage like bee balm and autumn chrysanthemums.

The thoughtfully planned scented garden will guarantee a feast of fragrant delights.

CHARLES DICKENS

The Bird Garden

BIRDS PLAY A key role in maintaining a balanced ecosystem. They help pollinate plants and trees and keep the insect population in check. But land development is making it increasingly difficult for birds to remain in their natural habitats. While birds can adapt to the changes in their environment, why not help by making your backyard bird-friendly?

Birds, like other animals, need food, water, and shelter. The bird garden can provide them all. And your new neighbors will continue to thank you in song.

When planting to provide food for the birds, follow one simple guideline: Include plants native to the area. After all, these are the ones local birds are used to having in their habitat. Visit a local nursery if unsure what is native, and plan to use as many plantings as the yard will allow.

Trees with berries, such as the American holly, sassafras, and crab apple, will provide birds with a year-round buffet. Birch trees and sunflowers will offer nuts and seeds. Some birds, such as orioles and hummingbirds, need nectar-producing plants. To attract these birds, plant indigenous flowers and flowering bushes. Keeping a pile of fallen leaves under a tree will encourage the presence of earthworms and other insects for the birds to feed on. And, of course, a bird feeder will provide additional treats regardless of season.

Water is important both for drinking and bathing. A birdbath works well to fill this need. A birdbath should be shallow enough for the smaller birds to stand in. Using one perched on a pedestal will also help keep the birds safe from predators. The birdbath should be kept clean and filled. In the winter, make sure the water in it doesn't freeze. You can do this by adding some warm water or by purchasing an electric warmer. Another solution is to keep the water circulating with a small pump so it won't freeze solid. That way the birds can have a much-needed drink even in the coldest weather. A small natural pond is also ideal for birds, but an ornamental pool or stream can also do the trick.

Birds need to nest and be protected from predators and inclement weather. Some birds nest on the ground, so planting prairie or ornamental grasses will furnish a habitat for them.

Ever wonder where a bird goes in a storm? Look in a conifer or any heavily branched evergreen.

These thick trees offer birds both a nesting place and weather protection. Yards that are too small for large evergreens can still contain birdhouses and nesting boxes. For best results, these houses need to be sized and constructed to the particular needs of the species in your area, so consult one of the many guides available to see which types of houses would be most beneficial.

Keeping birds safe from predators and environmental dangers can be a challenge. Positioning feeders, baths, and nesting boxes out of reach of cats is the first step to ensuring a safe haven. Try spraying white vinegar around the bath and feeders to keep the cats away. Brambles and other prickly plants will also keep birds safe from wandering paws, while at the same time providing food in the form of berries.

In addition to insects, birds eat fruits, nuts, and berries, so avoid spraying these plants with chemical pesticides. Not only do manicured lawns not provide much food or shelter for birds, but chemical applications of fertilizers and pesticides used for lawn growth can be extremely harmful to wildlife, especially birds. And resist the temptation to put feeders, baths, and nesting boxes near a window—birds sometimes can't distinguish glass from open sky and may fly into the window and be gravely injured.

Creating a garden as a natural haven for birds will benefit both the bird and the gardener. Bird song on a summer morning is reward enough.

CHARLES DICKENS

Rebecca

Suddenly he began to talk about Manderley. He said nothing of his life there, no word about himself, but he told me how the sun set there, on a spring afternoon, leaving a glow upon the headland. The sea would look like slate, cold still from the long winter, and from the terrace you could hear the ripple of the coming tide washing in the little bay. The daffodils were in bloom, stirring in the evening breeze, golden heads cupped upon lean stalks, and however many you might pick there would be no thinning of the ranks, they were massed like an army, shoulder to shoulder. On a bank below the lawns, crocuses were planted, golden, pink, and mauve, but by this time they would be past their best, dropping and fading, like the pallid snowdrops.

Suddenly I saw a clearing in the dark drive ahead, and a patch of sky, and in a moment the dark trees had thinned, the nameless shrubs had disappeared, and on either side of us was a wall of colour, blood-red, reaching far above our heads. We were amongst the rhododendrons. There was something bewildering, even shocking, about the suddenness of their discovery. The woods had not prepared me for them. They startled me with their crimson faces, massed one upon the other in incredible profusion, showing no leaf, no twig, nothing but the slaughterous red, luscious and fantastic, unlike any rhododendron plant I had seen before.

❧ *An Army of Daffodils* ❧

COLONIES OF DAFFODILS make a big splash when naturalized in sweeping drifts along roadsides, garden paths, and creek banks or across a field or yard. These sunny yellow flowers dress up plain patches of grass, especially under trees or on grassy banks. Grouped together informally and allowed to multiply freely, they create a profusion of golden cupped flowers.

The name daffodil comes from the English *Daffodyle* and means "early comer." While technically different, jonquils, narcissus, and daffodils are all members of the *Narcissus* genus, and are now commonly accepted as interchangeable names.

Daffodils are spring flowering bulbs and should be planted in the fall. The flowers are easy to care for and practically indestructible, happily grown in Zones 3 to 8. Thriving in a broad range of conditions, the bulbs require at least three weeks of cold winter weather (called dormancy) in order to set flower buds for the next year. Too-warm conditions will result in leaves and no blooms.

Consult with the local garden center to select a bulb that is comfortable in your zone and has a

good reputation for vigorous growth. Bulbs are also available at hardware stores and through mail-order catalogs, which will conveniently ship the bulbs to arrive at planting time. The bulbs should be planted as soon as possible to prevent drying, wilting, and scarring. If you are unable to plant them right away, store bulbs in a cool, dry place.

When naturalizing daffodils, it is important to go with the flow. Choose a spot with well-drained soil and at least half a day of sun. To create a ravishing display, plant just one kind. Scatter the bulbs generously across the chosen area in a broad, sweeping motion and plant them where they fall.

To plant the bulbs en masse, dig a trench, sprinkle some fertilizer in the bottom, and spread a dozen or more bulbs in the trench. Plant the bulbs close together, but not touching, for a dazzling effect. Gently replace the soil, taking care not to tip over the bulbs. Water thoroughly. Add a thick layer of mulch to keep the bulbs moist and to prevent weed growth.

Depending on the variety, the bulbs will flower between very early and late spring. After flowering, leave the clumps of bulbs until the leaves have withered. If your daffodils are in a highly visible spot and you find the dying foliage too messy, you can gather up and braid the leaves into a compact knot until they have died back and are ready to be removed.

Daffodils are divided among twelve types according to the shape of their cups and petals. Recommended varieties for naturalizing include:

- Trumpet daffodils, such as the yellow Arctic Gold and the white Beersheba
- Double daffodils, such as Acropolis, whose blooms are white with touches of red, and Ice King, which produces showy white flowers
- Large-cupped daffodils, such as Accent, which produces white and salmon-pink blooms
- Small-cupped, such as Edna Earl, with its blooms of white and orange
- *N. tazetta*, an easygoing variety that offers white, yellow, and orange flowers that will bloom as early as Christmas in areas with warm winters
- *N. Bulbocodium*, a popular wild daffodil with small yellow flowers with large cups
- *N. cyclamineus*, short yellow or yellow-and-white flowers that bloom very early in the spring
- *N. poeticus*, fragrant, tall, white-and-yellow, red-rimmed flowers that bloom at the end of the season (the famous daffodils of Wordsworth)
- *N. Triandrus*, whose stalks carry two or more blooms
- Miniature varieties are also a good option for gardeners with less space or who simply enjoy these sweet, tiny blossoms.

DAPHNE DU MAURIER

Daffodils are great cutting flowers, appropriate for simple bouquets or fancy arrangements. They also look magnificent in the garden. Plant a lot and then go ahead and pick as many as you like; your ranks will remain thick for years to come.

The Slaughterous Red Rhododendron

THE RHODODENDRON IS one of the easiest and most beautiful woodland shrubs to grow. Hardy and floriferous, this startlingly brilliant plant thrives in the partial shade of an open garden setting. There are hundreds of cultivars to choose from, from dwarf to giant varieties.

The rhododendron prefers a light, well-drained yet moist soil with high levels of organic matter. These evergreen bushes thrive in the Northwest and Northeast and are especially suited to Zones 5 and 6. Heavy or excessively wet or dry soils won't allow the roots to breathe and should be avoided. After planting, which can be done most any time with nursery-bought plants, apply a layer of mulch to retain moisture and prevent weed growth. Keep well watered throughout the first growing season and spray the plant with an anti-dessicant such as Wiltproof to prevent winter kill. After that, the plant should pretty much take care of itself.

The rhododendron is available in a spectacular variety of colors, ranging from pale yellows to shocking reds and purples. Depending on the variety, dense clusters of long-lasting blooms appear from early spring through early summer, with shrub sizes ranging from 3 to 20 feet. Compact varieties are an excellent choice for smaller garden areas, and are widely available at garden centers.

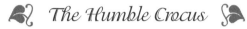 *The Humble Crocus*

ONE OF THE first signs of spring is the crocus peeking up through the ground after a long, hard winter. Spring crocuses bloom in March in the North, but the greens may start to appear as early as February if the weather is unexpectedly warm. The crocus is related to the iris and reaches about four to six inches in height, and is generally hardy from Zones 4 to 6, depending on the type. Crocuses come in many colors and varieties, are easy to plant and care for, and will provide years of bloom and pleasure from a single planting.

The bulbs of the spring crocus should be planted in October or November, before the ground freezes. The bulbs should be planted two to four inches deep and spaced about two inches apart. Plant crocuses in full sun in clusters of at least twenty to twenty-five for maximum effect, since the individual blooms are small. Crocuses can be planted in borders, in rock gardens, or in containers indoors or out. For the best blooms year after year, don't remove the leaves until they have died back, as they continue to provide nutrients to the bulb after the flower is gone.

Common types of spring crocuses, such as the Dutch crocus, come in assorted colors. The blue or purple varieties include Blue Pearl, Ruby Giant, Remembrance, and Pickwick, which is a purple-striped variety. White crocuses, like the Snowstorm or Cream Beauty set off the purple types beautifully.

Yellow Mammoth and Fusotinctus produce yellow blooms. Regardless of the variety used, water regularly, soaking the ground to allow the water to get to the bulb. Rodents like squirrels love the taste of crocus and often destroy the plants. To discourage this, sprinkle blood meal around the sprouting greens or keep a dog or cat handy!

The crocus is a small flower that can pack a mighty visual punch in any setting. Groups of crocuses clamor for attention along the sidewalk, under an apple tree, or in the center of a garden. The crocus may be humble, but it is one of the first and best heralds of spring and deserves a spot in every garden.

The Mill on the Floss

"O may I get this rose?" said Maggie, making a great effort to say something, and dissipate the burning sense of irretrievable confession. "I think I am quite wicked with roses—I like to gather them and smell them till they have no scent left."

Stephen was mute: he was incapable of putting a sentence together, and Maggie bent her arm a little upward towards the large half-opened rose that had attracted her. Who has not felt the beauty of a woman's arm?— the unspeakable suggestions of tenderness that lie in the dimpled elbow and all the varied gently lessening curves

down to the delicate wrist with its tiniest, almost imperceptible nicks in the firm softness. A woman's arm touched the soul of a great sculptor two thousand years ago, so that he wrought an image of it for the Parthenon which moves us still as it clasps lovingly the time-worn marble of a headless trunk. Maggie's was such an arm as that—and it had the warm tints of life.

A mad impulse seized on Stephen; he darted towards the arm, and showered kisses on it, clasping the wrist.

Wicked with Roses

THROUGH LOVING CARE, the beloved queen of the garden—the rose—will nourish your spirit and offer fragrant beauty beyond compare, year after year. The rose, a cherished favorite cultivated throughout the world for centuries, is actually fairly easy to grow. And today, there are literally thousands of cultivars from which to choose.

The hardiness of roses is affected by temperature fluctuations, dry or soggy soil, wind, and other factors, so be sure to choose a variety that is known to grow well in your area. When choosing a plant, take into consideration its shape, growth habits, blooming season, and disease resistance, in addition to the way its flowers look.

Roses should be planted near the house where their fragrance can filter through open windows, across front porches, and over walkways. All roses enjoy a sheltered, sunny site with well-drained, friable soil near a water source. Good air circulation is also important; avoid shade and wet soils.

To plant, first dig a large hole—make it larger than it seems it should be. Save the first half of the dirt you remove and discard the rest. Next, fill the hole with a large amount of organic matter, such as aged cow or horse manure, compost, and seaweed. Mix these amendments with the saved dirt and some phosphorous (0-46-0), and fill the hole almost full. Set the rose bush so the graft union is three inches below the final grade, and completely fill in the hole. Water thoroughly, and saucer the hole so that water will sink in and not run off. Finish by covering the planted area with a blanket of mulch.

Watering is essential. A layer of mulch will help by conserving moisture and controlling weeds. Fertilize the bushes each spring with composted animal manure. During the blooming season, feed the roses every four to six weeks with a balanced granular formulation of nitrogen, phosphorus, and potassium. And keep the faded blooms picked—a process called deadheading—throughout the season. Watch for signs of pests or disease.

Prune in late winter to early spring, after the nips have had a chance to form. Using sharp pruning shears, remove all old or diseased canes. This will maintain good air circulation and improve the

GEORGE ELIOT

health of the plant. To prepare for winter in cold zones, protect the bushes with a warm blanket of mulch, leaves, or hay.

Some popular fragrant roses include the hardy, deep pink Carefree Beauty, which produces rose hips in the fall; the less hardy but very perfumed, scarlet-flowered Don Juan; the hardy white Iceberg; the bushy English variety Mary Rose; and the hardy hybrid Penelope.

Whatever variety you choose, your roses will be stalwarts in the garden, offering beauty, perfume, and a spiritual boost.

Thus we came to the garden, where I had never been before. It was a great square, shut in with a brick wall of twelve or fifteen feet, big enough to suit a palace, but then ill kept and sorely over-grown. I could spend long in speaking of that plot; how the flowers, and fruit-trees, pot-herbs, spice, and simples ran all wild and intermixed. The pink brick walls caught every ray of sun that fell, and that morning there was a hushed, close heat in it, and a warm breath rose from the strawberry beds, for they were then in full bearing. I was glad enough to get out of the sun when Grace led the way into a walk of medlar trees and quinces, where the boughs interlaced and formed an alley to a brick summer-house. This summer-house stands in the angle of the south wall, and by it two old fig-trees, whose tops you can see from the outside. They are well known for the biggest and earliest-bearing of all that part, and Grace showed me how, if danger threatened, I might climb up their boughs and scale the wall.

QUINCE IS GROWN mostly in temperate regions, in zones 4 to 8, and can reach heights up to 15 feet. There are two species of plant popularly called quince: one bearing fruit *(Cydonia oblonga)* and the other flowers *(Chaenomoles sp.)*. The fruit-bearer is actually a small tree (up to 24 feet) and produces a tart, pear-shaped quince covered with fuzz. The flowering species presents its one-inch-wide pink or white blossoms in late spring.

The flowering quince is a favorite for winter bouquets because it can be forced to bloom indoors.

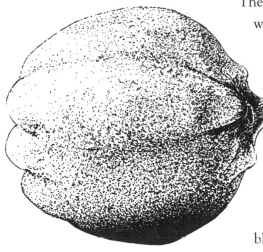

The dark, angular branches are punctuated with flowers from white through red, depending on the species; they have an Oriental look, and are gracious in appearance.

Forcing quince is simple. At any time from late January through March, snip a few branches and immediately place the stalks in a vase filled with warm water in a warm room. Soaking the branches overnight in a bathtub of warm water will speed the process. This will loosen the buds, enabling them to open sooner. Keep in mind that the earlier in the season you cut the branches, the longer they will take to bloom.

Outdoors, the quince bush is easy to grow and should be planted in humus-rich ground. It requires a sunny garden position and appreciates protection from the cold. Once established, quince needs little care. Keep the plant well watered during hot, dry summers. Apply an even blanket of manure or compost each spring.

Quince trees will begin to bear fruit after their fourth or fifth year; trees are self-fruitful, so you only need one to produce a bountiful crop. Care and culture are similar to pears and apples.

Quince fruit grows on the tips of the branches of the current season's growth. Pruning will stimulate branching, which will enhance the formation of new growth and increase fruit production and flowering. But prune carefully. In winter, remove old, overcrowded growth. Don't remove every lateral growth, or you'll be getting rid of next season's fruit. Keep the branches thinned and remove crossing branches and deadwood so the plant can receive more sun.

Quince is occasionally susceptible to a disease known as fire blight, a result of excessive nitrogen additives. This is evident by black or brown foliage that shrivels up and dies, clinging to the stem. To control the spread of this disease, prune out the infected area to twenty-four inches beyond the damage. (Make sure to disinfect the pruner before using it again.) Stemrust and oriental fruit moths can also be a problem, so spray appropriately, if necessary.

The fruit will easily separate from the tree and release a strong, fragrant aroma when it is fully ripe and ready for harvest. Pick the fruit when the skins have turned from green to gold and the fruit is between two and a half and four inches in size. Don't store quince with other fruits; the strong odor will spoil them. Store them separately in boxes in a cool, well-ventilated area. Don't wrap them, or they will discolor. The fruit can't be eaten raw, but can be used in pies and tarts. Common cultivars include, Champion, Orange, Portugal, and Smyrna.

J. MEADE FALKNER

Quince Marmalade

THE QUINCE, THOUGH highly esteemed abroad, is somewhat of a mystery in the United States. The ancient Greeks and Romans deemed it the symbol of love. Some even believe it was a quince that Eve gave Adam in the Garden of Eden. Closely related to the apple and pear, it stands up well to long cooking and is well suited for marmalade, jam, or pie. It has a green to yellow skin color, and the skin is quite hard. The curious thing about quince is that when it cooks, the pale flesh becomes a pinkish color, lending interest to any recipe that calls for apples. Quinces, which have an acidic flavor, aren't usually eaten raw. As the color changes while cooking, the flavor becomes sweeter and mellower. Specialty grocers and produce markets are carrying more quinces each year. They are in season in the late fall, so look for them during the holiday season. Choose quinces that are large, firm, and aromatic. They can be kept stored in the refrigerator for up to three weeks.

4 quinces
3 cups water
2 cups sugar
¼ cup lemon rind
3 tablespoons fresh lemon juice

Peel, core, and chop the quinces. Add all ingredients to a large saucepan. Combine well and bring to a boil. Reduce heat and cook 1¼ hours or until thick. Cool the mixture. Store in an airtight container for up to two weeks in the refrigerator.

YIELD: 2½ cups

THE COMMON FIG, or *Ficus carica*, can be grown as a bush or small tree. It produces abundant rich, sweet fruit ranging in color from deep purple to yellowish white that can be added fresh or dried to other fruits, cereals, salads, stews, and desserts or simply eaten alone. Figs provide a tasty and easy way to enhance the nutritional value of your daily fare. They are also used medicinally in the preparation of laxatives.

Indigenous to Persia, Asia Minor, and Syria, this delicious fruit is mentioned frequently in the Bible. It now grows wild, thriving in the hot, dry summer sun of many Mediterranean countries, Europe, and the United States. Highly nutritious, it was a principle item of sustenance for the Greeks and used largely by the Spartans and the first Olympians, who believed it gave them speed and endurance. What we consider the "fruit" of the fig really isn't, botanically speaking. Something of a horticultural oddity, the fruit is actually a receptacle which houses the true fruits, which most people consider the seeds. It takes two to three growing seasons for a young fig tree to bear fruit, but once it begins, it can produce up to a hundred years.

Figs can be grown outdoors as far north as Zones 7 and 8, and in movable tubs in colder areas that can be wintered in basements or garages. To start, choose a two-year-old, potted specimen and plant it in a sunny, sheltered spot in the spring after danger of frost has passed. The soil should be friable, rich, and well drained. Avoid wet areas where water collects to prevent excessive growth (overproduction compromises the quality of the fruit). Gently loosen the roots from the soil ball before planting. The plant can be trained to cover a wall using a technique called espaliering, by pruning the main stem to a height of one foot and allowing a shoot to grow on either side. To fertilize, cover the base of the plant

J. MEADE FALKNER

with a layer of well-rotted manure or fertilizer each spring. Apply supplemental feedings during the summer months, but take care not to overfertilize. Watering is necessary during hot, dry spells. In Zone 7 and the northern portion of Zone 8, it is usually best to lay the tree on the ground and cover with soil for winter protection.

Scale is the major problem with figs. Use insecticidal soap or spray to control. White fly, aphids and red spider mites can also be a problem, but are easily controlled by chemical or biological means.

Figs grown in mild climates require little pruning. In the spring, shorten spreading branches to more vertical shoots and leave some growth in the middle of the tree to protect it from exposure to the sun. In colder areas, prune all crossing or damaged branches, keep the center open by eliminating upright shoots, and prune to buds on lower branches.

Harvest the pear-shaped fruits when they have fully ripened, becoming soft to the touch. The skins may split open and the branches will hang down.

Propagation can be done by cultivating hardwood cuttings. Insert the cuttings in well-prepared soil in a protected area.

Fig varieties can be chosen according to when in the growing season they bear their fruit. Common types include:

Early: Celeste, Osborne Prolific, White Marseilles
Midseason: Alma, Brown Turkey, Brunswick
Late: Conadria

Tender Is the Night

Feeling good from the rosy wine at lunch, Nicole Diver folded her arms high enough for the artificial camellia on her shoulder to touch her cheek, and went out into her lovely grassless garden. The garden was bounded on one side by the house, from which it flowed and into which it ran, on two sides by the old village, and on the last by the cliff falling by ledges to the sea.

Along the walls on the village side all was dusty, the wriggling vines, the lemon and eucalyptus trees, the casual wheel-barrow, left only a moment since, but already grown into the path, atrophied and faintly rotten. Nicole was invariably somewhat surprised that by turning in the other direction past a bed of peonies she walked into an area so green and cool that the leaves and petals were curled with tender damp.

Knotted at her throat she wore a lilac scarf that ever in the achromatic sunshine cast its color up to her face and down around her moving feet in a lilac shadow. Her face was hard, almost stern, save for the soft gleam of piteous doubt that looked from her green eyes. Her once fair hair had darkened, but she was lovelier now at twenty-four than she had been at eighteen, when her hair was brighter than she.

Following a walk marked by an intangible mist of bloom that followed the white border stones she came to a space overlooking the sea where there were lanterns asleep in the fig trees and a big table and wicker chairs and a great market umbrella from Sienna, all gathered about an enormous pine, the biggest tree in the garden. She paused there a moment, looking absently at a growth of nasturtiums and iris tangled at its foot, as though sprung from a careless handful of seeds, listening to the plaints and accusations of some nursery squabble in the house. When this died away on the summer air, she walked on, between kaleidoscopic peonies massed in pink clouds, black and brown tulips and fragile mauve-stemmed roses, transparent like sugar flowers in a confectioner's window— until, as if the scherzo of color could reach no further intensity, it broke off suddenly in mid-air, and moist steps went down to a level five feet below.

Here there was a well with the boarding around it dank and slippery even on the brightest days. She went up the stairs on the other side and into the vegetable garden; she walked rather quickly; she liked to be active, though at times she gave an impression of repose that was at once static and evocative.

Nicole Diver's Summer Garden

NICOLE DIVER IS an ethereal soul, and her garden is awash in scent and diaphanous drama. Set in Nice, her seaside garden enjoys intense sunlight here, a shady, moist environment there, and those delicious nooks and crannies that allow for rampant growth of flowering vines and such. Nicole is surely more the appreciative audience for her "lovely grassless garden" than the gardener within it. She wanders the dusty gravel or crushed shell paths, allowing each of the plantings to surprise and delight her, as well they should.

If a garden is a room, then the trees in Nicole's garden are her unusual collection of exquisite furniture. First, the lemon tree, which provides luscious bursts of scent throughout the year; next the eucalyptus, a splendid creature clothed in bluish, fragrant leaves. Even the fig trees, with their sweet, vaguely erotic fruit, and the tall, rigid pines add a sense of mystery and romance to an already bewitching location. These "pieces" are each enhanced by the distinctive "appointments," such as the nasturtiums, peonies, tulips, and roses. Small "bibelots" in the form of an old barrow and white border stones complete the scene. In this magical setting, not one of these plantings is ordinary: Each seems an effortless part of the stylish whole—a gardener's dream come true.

Not many of us enjoy such lush and unique features in our gardens—a mossy well or a border comprised of cliffs and the sea. But we capture a bit of Nicole Diver's élan, as well as the romance of her garden. A big country table, wicker chairs, and a market umbrella are within our grasp, thanks to purveyors of outdoor fashion such as Gardener's Eden, Smith & Hawken, and even the Pottery Barn. A lemon tree in a big terra-cotta pot could add a seasonal dash of the Mediterranean to a sunny porch or terrace. And tulips or roses in arresting colors are just a phone call away, thanks to Whiteflower Farm and others.

Finally, take a truly useful cue from Nicole Diver and make a point of simply walking around your garden from time to time, as if you're the host of a party trying to enjoy a moment with each and every guest. It's a great exercise, because you notice and appreciate different things in your garden when you behave as a spectator rather than a participant—and you'll remind yourself of why you garden in the first place.

F. SCOTT FITZGERALD

127

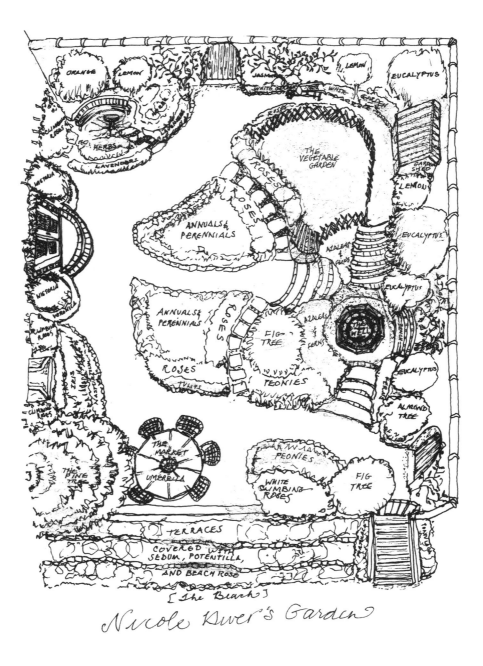

Nicole River's Garden

Nicole Diver's Garden

PERENNIALS

Iris
Lily
Delphinium
Coreopsis
Poppy
Dianthus
Lady's Mantle
Foxglove
Aster
Valerian

VINES

Trumpet-Vine
Jasmine
Clematis
Morning-Glory

WHITE GARDEN

Artemisia
Lamb's Ear
Silver Sage
Silver Horehound
Snow-in-Summer
Spotted Dead Nettle
Ghost Plant
Pearly Everlasting
Pinks

HERBS

Thyme
(Path with
   creeping Thyme)
Rosemary
Chives
Tarragon
Sweet Woodruff
Lavender
Cat-Mint
Mint
Monarda

ANNUALS

Sunflower
Poppy
Cosmos
Snapdragon
Daisy
Petunia

The Kaleidoscopic Peonies

THE PEONY, A native of China, is a garden classic that dutifully fulfills the promises of spring. The red wine–colored shoots of this fragrant beauty emerge from the earth slowly, unfolding into a display of luscious blossoms. If properly cared for, the peony will blossom for decades. And, when all the flowers are gone, the dark green foliage retains its rich color and provides a lovely background for other flowers until the first frost.

Fall is the best time to plant bare-root plants; container-grown peonies should be purchased and planted in the spring. Peonies are hardy souls and can be easily grown in Zones 3 through 8 and along the West Coast. The plants will reach a height of three to four feet.

Choose a site with well-drained soil in full sun. Dig a large hole approximately two feet deep and enrich the soil with well-aged compost and well-rotted manure. Set the plant in the soil so the top of the bud is no more than two inches below the soil surface. Fertilize twice a year in early spring and again in the fall. Sprinkle a handful of bone meal around each plant and scratch into the soil.

Early staking is highly recommended since the opened flowers droop under the weight of heavy spring rain. An assortment of staking apparatuses is available and can be found at the local garden center. You can also fashion your own from chicken wire. Simply cut a round piece and place over the spears when they first appear. As the plant matures, lift the chicken wire. This is an economical way to keep the pretty faces of the peonies from lying in patches of damp earth.

Patience is a virtue when growing peonies. The plants will begin to blossom in the second year and take several years to attain full size. But once established, this gem of a flower will create a magical, perfumed elegance in your garden for decades to come.

Peonies produce single and double blossoms in a wide range of colors—from pristine white and pale pink to sunny yellow and blushing red—early, mid, and late in the season. By carefully selecting from each of these varieties you can enjoy a splashy display and delicious aroma from spring through early summer. Some noted favorites include:

Early: Buckeye Belle Hybrid, Red Charm, and Single Friendship Hybrid
Midseason: Gardenia, Douglas Brand, and Hermione
Late: Japanese Nippon Beauty, Monsieur DuPont, and Gibraltar

The Accidental Ornament

AN OVERTURNED WHEELBARROW, faintly rotten, becomes part of the garden path itself. It might not seem a likely garden ornament, but this chance meeting of nature and object create a casual style of decoration.

While the wheelbarrow may be forgotten accidentally in the garden, deliberate placement of objects around the yard can create an offhand look. Articles that are related to the yard and garden are a natural choice for this style of decoration. A French watering can left at the corner of the flower bed or a period croquet set leaning against a tree in the yard are examples. An antique garden tool set in a wicker basket, balanced on a stone wall or garden table, makes a fanciful accent to enhance the garden. You can punctuate with color, say, with a pair of bright red garden clogs or yellow rain boots lounging against the potting bench. And instead of throwing broken garden decorations away, use cracked or collapsed statues and birdbaths as a support for all kinds of plant life.

In the same way such carefully placed objects create a stylish atmosphere within the home, so they do outside the home. This "accidental" style of decoration is just part of the fine art of garden design. A visitor will be surprised by how easily these sorts of objects blend with the surroundings. The article by itself isn't the actual ornament; it's the relationship between the object and the garden that is the secret to this touch.

The dog-roses are too sweet. There is a great hedge of them over the lawn—magnificently tall, so that they fall down in garlands, and nice and thin at the bottom, so that you can see ducks through it and a cow. These belong to the farm, which is the only house near us. There goes the breakfast gong. Much love. Modified love to Tibby. Love to Aunt Juley; how good of her to come and keep you company, but what a bore. Burn this. Will write again Thursday.

"HELEN."

THE DOG ROSE, *Rosa canina,* is an ideal choice for a woodland hedge or country setting. One of the oldest rose cultivars, this beautiful wild bloomer dates to the ninth century and is esteemed for its hips, which are rich in vitamin C.

Single white or pink blossoms are borne in small clusters on twining vines that reach heights up to ten feet. The dog rose performs beautifully in Zone 5 and is hardy to Zone 4.

Also known as wild briar, the dog rose produces rose hips, the fruit that develops after the flower fades, which can be used in making jellies, candies, syrup, soup, and other recipes. Rose hips can also be found in vitamin tablets and herbal remedies. And the dried leaves of the dog rose can be used to make tea.

Dog roses are available through specialty mail-order catalogs and full-venue garden centers. The beauty of this ancient cultivar makes it worth the search.

Where Angels Fear to Tread

They sowed the duller vegetables first, and a pleasant feeling of righteous fatigue stole over them as they addressed themselves to the peas. Harriet stretched a string to guide the row straight, and Mrs. Herriton scratched a furrow with a pointed stick. At the end of it she looked at her watch.

"It's twelve! The second post's in. Run and see if there are any letters."

Harriet did not want to go. "Let's finish the peas. There won't be any letters."

"No, dear; please go. I'll sow the peas, but you shall cover them up—and mind the birds don't see 'em!"

Mrs. Herriton was very careful to let those peas trickle evenly from her hand, and at the end of the row she was conscious that she had never sown better. They were expensive too.

❧ The Pea Patch ❧

WHAT SPRING VEGETABLE garden would be complete without a crop of peas? This tiny delicacy is an annual garden favorite.

There are three general categories to choose from: English peas, edible-pod peas, and snap peas. English peas are shelling peas whose pods are inedible. Edible-pod peas are just as the name suggests—peas within pods that can be eaten. This type includes sugar peas and snow peas. Snap peas are sweet and delicious and can be "snapped" directly into salads or eaten whole while standing in the garden.

Peas grow on a slender, twining vine that reaches from four to six feet tall and most need to be supported by a wire or twine frame, trellis, or fence.

Varieties available range from early-, mid-, and late-season to dwarf. Look for English varieties Alaska, Lincoln, and dwarf Little Marvel. Favorite snap varieties include Sugar Snap and Sugar Ann. A couple of edible-pod types to try are Sugar Pod and Dwarf Sugar.

Sow seeds directly into the ground as soon as the soil can be worked. Consult your local nursery or almanac to find the correct date for your area. Sow at bi-weekly intervals to stagger harvest time. Plant seeds one to two inches deep, one inch apart, and in rows two feet apart. The supports should be installed at the time of planting to avoid disturbing the roots later. Germination will occur in one to three weeks. Peas can also be planted in double rows spaced six inches apart with three feet between each set of double rows. Peas are also a good crop for the fall and should be sown three months prior to the first frost date.

Keep peas watered and weeded. Fertilizer should be used sparingly. Excessive amounts of nitrogen will cause an overgrowth of foliage and weaken pea production.

E. M. FORSTER

Typically, peas should be harvested at their peak, approximately sixty to seventy days after planting. Harvest time will vary according to variety. Pick English peas when they are plump and round. Edible-pod peas should be harvested when the pods are soft, tender, and edible and before they begin to accumulate a lot of starch. They will still be slender and two to three inches long.

Snap peas can be allowed to mature without the pods becoming too tough. Sugar snaps will be at their peak when the pod is two and a half to three inches long and has begun to swell and the individual peas are just discernable.

Keep the vines picked each day during harvest to encourage fruit production. If the vines aren't kept picked, fruit production will cease. Peas left on the vine become tasteless, mushy, and stringy, and then are only good for the compost heap.

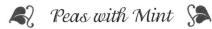

Peas with Mint

FRESH SWEET PEAS are readily available in produce markets and grocery stores in the spring. Whether picked from the garden or bought at the market, plan on using them the same day. Look for pods that are bright green and snap apart rather than give when bent. Some varieties of fresh peas may need to be shelled before cooking; simply open the pod and ease the peas out. In most recipes, frozen peas may be substituted, but they won't offer the same intense flavor and texture as fresh peas. Do not overcook fresh peas; their beauty is in the color and crunchiness. If fresh peas will be cooked again in part of a recipe, blanch them for one minute in boiling salted water before adding them to the other ingredients. Many people prefer to use them just blanched in any recipe.

3 cups fresh peas, shelled
1 tablespoon butter
1 to 2 tablespoons chopped fresh mint, to taste
1 teaspoon grated lemon peel
½ teaspoon sugar
½ teaspoon salt
Pepper, to taste

Cook the peas in boiling salted water for about three to four minutes. Melt the butter in a large saucepan. Add the mint, lemon peel, sugar, salt, and pepper to taste. Mix well. Add the peas to the sauce, just to heat them through. Serve immediately.

YIELD: 6 servings

E. M. FORSTER

The Return of the Native

Yeobright did not interrupt the preparations, and went home again. The next morning, when Thomasin withdrew the curtains of her bedroom window, there stood the Maypole in the middle of the green, its top cutting into the sky. It had sprung up in the night, or rather early morning, like Jack's bean stalk. She opened the casement to get a better view of the garlands and posies that adorned it. The sweet perfume of the flowers had already spread into the surrounding air, which, being free from every taint, conducted to her lips a full measure of the fragrance received from the spire of blossom in its midst. At the top of the pole were crossed hoops decked with small flowers; beneath these came a milk-white zone of Maybloom; then a zone of bluebells, then of cowslips, then of lilacs, then of ragged-robins, daffodils, and so on, till the lowest stage was reached. Thomasin noticed all these, and was delighted that the May revel was to be so near.

When afternoon came people began to gather on the green, and Yeobright was interested enough to look out upon them from the open window of his room. Soon after this Thomasin walked out from the door immediately below and turned her eyes up to her cousin's face. She was dressed more gaily than Yeobright had ever seen her dressed since the time of Wildeve's death, eighteen months before; since the day of her marriage even she had not exhibited herself to such advantage.

The Lost Art of Making a Maypole

MAY DAY, TRADITIONALLY celebrated May 1, originated as a pagan Roman holiday that honored the flower goddess, Flora. Roman children would decorate a large marble column in Flora's temple with twining garlands of flowers.

Long after the departure of the legions, the celebrations continued throughout the former Empire, especially in England. There, branches were removed from the trunk of a tall tree, which was placed as a centerpiece in the village square and festooned with garlands of flowers in early spring. English children, dressed in their spring finery, wove ribbons and flowers around the maypole as they danced and sang to herald the arrival of spring. The maypole was often topped with the flag of Great Britain, striped with colorful ribbons, and layered with festive flower wreaths.

Great competition existed among the villages to find the tallest pole. A fir tree was often used, as was a ship's mast. The London maypole became a familiar sight in the city for many years until the festival was halted by the Puritans. However, the maypole and the tradition of bidding farewell to the winter was not easily destroyed. It became known as the May Tree and, in France during the revolution, as the Tree of Liberty.

Whatever its symbol's name, May Day is a perfect time to gather friends and family to rejoice in the wonders of a new spring.

Decorating and raising a maypole takes a little planning, but the sight and scents that surround the finished product are well worth it. The basis of the maypole is, of course, the pole itself. This can be a tall tree with a few branches already growing in the yard, or a classic maypole can be fashioned from a fir sapling stripped of all but the topmost branches. If cutting down a tree isn't an option, use a large dowel, pole, or tall clothesline pole.

A maypole should be nine to twelve feet high with an additional 2–3 feet for anchoring it into the ground. Dig a large hole, insert the maypole, secure the base with some large, heavy stones, and fill with the remaining dirt. Always test the maypole to make sure it's sturdy and won't tip over when the ribbons are pulled around it: a little concrete may be poured in the hole for added security.

Decorating the maypole with flowers and flowing ribbons is the fun part. The top of the maypole can be adorned with a garland of fresh flowers and greenery such as ferns. Use the most fragrant flowers, and gather them on the morning of the festivities so they'll stay fresh and fragrant. The ribbons should be attached in multiples of four, depending on the number of dancers. They need to be one and one half times as long as the pole itself to allow for the winding during the dance. Use spring colors in the maypole scheme: green, soft pink, blue, and yellow are good choices. For an added bit of color, attach more flowers to the ends of the ribbons.

Traditionally, children perform the maypole dance, but there's no reason adults can't join in. Dancers are divided into two groups, and each dancer holds a ribbon. Half form the inner circle—nearest the pole—and half make up the outer circle. There are two basic types of maypole dances. One is the closed plait, in which the ribbons are simply wound around the pole itself. An example of this is "The Barber's Pole," a striped pattern that coils down the pole. Another more complicated dance is "Plait the Rope," in which the group of four outer dancers braids its ribbons around the ribbons of the inner dancers, creating ropes that hang from the maypole.

There may be a bit of confusion during the first maypole dance, but keep at it. Creating a simple barber-pole design leaves a colorful pattern to be admired. Go out and pick the newly blooming flowers, settle back with family and friends, and experience the splendor of the new season.

NATHANIEL HAWTHORNE

The Blithedale Romance

Long since, in this part of our circumjacent wood, I had found out for myself a little hermitage. It was a kind of leafy cave, high upward into the air, among the midmost branches of a white-pine tree. A wild grapevine, of unusual size and luxuriance, had twined and twisted itself up into the tree, and, after wreathing the entanglement of its tendrils around almost every bough, had caught hold of three or four neighboring trees, and married the whole clump with a perfectly inextricable knot of polygamy. Once, while sheltering myself from a summer shower, the fancy had taken me to clamber up into this seemingly impervious mass of foliage. The branches yielded me a passage, and closed again, beneath, as if only a squirrel or a bird had passed. Far aloft, around the stem of the central pine, behold, a perfect nest for Robinson Crusoe or King Charles! A hollow chamber, of rare seclusion, had been formed by the decay of some of the pine-branches, which the vine had lovingly strangled with its embrace, burying them from the light of day in an aerial sepulchre of its own leaves. It cost me but little ingenuity to enlarge the interior, and open loop-holes through the verdant walls. Had it ever been my fortune to spend a honey-moon, I should have thought seriously of inviting my bride up thither, where our next neighbors would have been two orioles in another part of the clump.

❧ Cleverly Climbing Vines ❧

CLIMBING VINES CARRY the glory of summer through the heart of winter. They create an other-world quality, inviting mystery, drama, and intrigue to the garden as they ramble over arbors and fences, along paths, and up mailboxes.

Most vines are a snap to grow and take up little space, but they do need supports. Luckily, the vines will attach themselves to just about anything that lies in their path. The tops of the plants should reach the sunshine, but their roots prefer to be planted in rich soil and covered in shade.

Annual and perennial varieties (some evergreen) produce rich harvests of flowers in a full spectrum of colors, edible fruits, and overwhelming fragrance. There is a vine for every occasion.

Annuals are a good choice for quick coverage. Consider the morning glory, hyacinth bean, scarlet runner bean, nasturtium, or sweet pea. Perennials sometimes take a year or two to become established, but from then on they will remain a stalwart in the garden. These include clematis, trumpet vine, wisteria, honeysuckle, and mandevilla.

Evergreens move to center stage in winter. They are sure, strong, and lasting. The evergreen vines include winter creeper, ivy, and bittersweet, and winter jasmine. (Be sure to check the hardiness of various vines to make sure they are adapted to your garden.) Although they don't bear flowers, they will reward the gardener with their deep-green seasonal color. Often used as ground covers, evergreens can be trained to any support, decorating the landscape long after most other plants have left the stage.

❧ Climb a Tree ❧

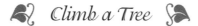

WANT TO GET a bird's-eye view? Climb a tree. Find the perfect perch to survey the land, observe a backyard gathering, spy on the neighborhood, or hide from Mom's calls to a dinner of liver and onions.

While children have always found the pull to the higher branches of just about any tree irresistible, many adults are now finding their own spirit of adventure and joining in.

The best trees to climb are ones with sturdy branches. Taller trees with more sparse branches may require the use of special climbing equipment. Hoisting oneself up to the first branch is probably the most challenging part; gravity—or those extra fifteen pounds you've put on since college—may be working against you, but keep trying. Once you're settled on the first branch, find foot- and handholds to maneuver around the tree. Keep a close eye out for bees and hornets, and stay away from birds' nests. Keep a firm grip on the branches while exploring the tree; you're never on quite as solid a footing as you think you are. Climbing down calls for the same strategies, but in reverse. Be sure to have a good foothold on a branch before putting your full weight on it.

Believe it or not, there are some organized tree-climbing clubs that host beginner and weekend tree-climbing excursions. This type of tree-climbing is serious, with ropes and harnesses for safety. These climbers reach great heights and get hooked on finding the most challenging climbs. They also work to perfect the art of branch walking and tree-to-tree traverses, and even indulge in overnight treetop camping.

You can become a treetop photographer, birdwatcher, or journalist if you really catch the bug. Or if you're just looking for a little peace and quiet, climb the nearest tree and become one with the branches. You'll get a new perspective on life with an exhilarating, peaceful view from the top.

For more information on tree-climbing clubs, tree-climbing equipment, and tree-climbing excursions, contact:

Tree Climbers International
PO Box 5588
Atlanta, GA 30307
(404) 377-9663
www.treeclimbing.com

NATHANIEL HAWTHORNE

"Rappaccini's Daughter"

Giovanni still found no better occupation than to look down into the garden beneath his window. From its appearance, he judged it to be one of those botanic gardens which were of earlier date in Padua than elsewhere in Italy or in the world. Or, not improbably, it might once have been the pleasure place of an opulent family; for there was the ruin of a marble fountain in the center, sculptured with rare art, but so woefully shattered that it was impossible to trace the original design from the chaos of remaining fragments. The water, however, continued to gush and sparkle into the sunbeams as cheerfully as ever. A little gurgling sound ascended to the young man's window, and made him feel as if the fountain were an immortal spirit that sung its song unceasingly and without heeding the vicissitudes around it, while one century embodied it in marble and another scattered the perishable garniture on the soil. All about the pool into which the water subsided grew various plants, that seemed to require a plentiful supply of moisture for the nourishment of gigantic leaves, and, in some instances, flowers gorgeously magnificent. There was one shrub in particular, set in a marble vase in the midst of the pool, that bore a profusion of purple blossoms, each of which had the luster and richness of a gem; and the whole together made a show so resplendent that it seemed enough to illuminate the garden, even had there been no sunshine. Every portion of the soil was peopled with plants and herbs, which, if less beautiful, still bore tokens of assiduous care, as if all had their individual virtues, known to the scientific mind that fostered them. Some were placed in urns, rich with old carving, and others in common garden pots; some crept serpent-like along the ground or climbed on high, using whatever means of ascent was offered them. One plant had wreathed itself round a statue of Vertumnus, which was thus quite veiled and shrouded in a drapery of hanging foliage, so happily arranged that it might have served a sculptor for a study.

NATHANIEL HAWTHORNE

149

GIOVANNI GUASCONTI HAD the best—and deadliest—view in town. And it was all the more appreciated as he looked down onto its riches from his own dingy rooms. From there he could see this rich botanic garden in all its overripe, overflowing splendor. He could also see Beatrice, the impossibly beautiful daughter of his neighbor, Dottore Rappaccini, as she tenderly doted on the inhabitants of her father's garden.

The Italian botanic garden's primary design was to cultivate plants for medicinal purposes. So it would certainly make sense that the doctor's garden would be filled with powerful and unusual specimens worthy of his study. The botanic garden was also meant to be an encyclopedic collection of plants from all over the world, the horticultural equivalent of a deluxe stamp collection. Rappaccini's lush garden was that and more.

The idea that Rappaccini cultivated poisonous plants is not based in fantasy. History is filled with poison plant aficionados, from the ancient Greeks to the Borgias and de Medicis. As a common sort of man, Giovanni was blithely unaware of the fact of such collections and certainly didn't know the identity of the mysterious purple flower in the marble vase set in the garden's fountain. This flower was likely either monkshood, whose beauty is notorious but which is known to be mortally toxic to humans and animals; or it was aconite, a witchly plant (and Medea's favorite, as it happens) of devastating beauty.

The "profusion of purple blossoms" proved Giovanni's helpless undoing. One can't help wondering how he allowed himself to be lured into a garden which featured shattered ruins, plants which "crept serpent-like along the ground," and a statue of Vertumnus, a mythological fellow who also fell hard for the charms of a mysterious woman and her garden. After all, how many warning signs can one man ignore? All of them, it would seem.

 Garden Ornament and Sculpture

ORNAMENTATION AND SCULPTURE bring structure and fun to the garden. They can be used to direct the eye by creating a focal point, as an enticement to meander down a path, or just to coax a smile. Clever use of accents and embellishments soften harsh lines, enhance landscapes, and adorn undesirable spaces. Open your mind and throw away conventionality. Any object can become a part of your statuary—it doesn't have to be an estate survivor. Consider sculptures, sundials, birdhouses, urns, grottos, topiary figures, wall ornaments, water baths, flowering vines, and potted plants. Use ornamentation in your garden to define yourself and create your own place. The possibilities are endless.

Just use your good judgment and consider these concerns:

- Is it appropriate to the setting?
- Is the scale right?
- Is the line appealing to your eye?
- Is the color right?
- Is it durable? Will it stand up to the elements?

Haunt flea markets, junk shops, tag sales. Chips, rust, and imperfections give an object instant history and a timeless richness. Craft shops abound that offer instructions and materials to give objects that aged look. There can be no better pastime, in the early morning or at the end of a long day, than to survey a garden that expresses your own personality.

The Mystery of Vertumnus

WHEN THE SEASONS change and the leaves on the trees turn from green to gold and scarlet, think of Vertumnus, the Roman deity of seasons and changes. Just as the leaves change their appearance, Vertumnus had the power to transform himself into various forms. He was very cunning in his use of this power, as the story of Vertumnus and Pomona proves.

Pomona was the Roman goddess of the fruit of the trees. She kept a luxurious garden and tenderly cared for every plant. Pomona was beautiful, and many suitors tried to win her love. She ignored them all, showering her love on only her garden. Vertumnus was in love with Pomona also, but he was more persistent than the rest. Pomona allowed no men in her garden, so Vertumnus used his powers to change himself into an old woman. When he was allowed into the garden, he proceeded to craft a story for Pomona.

Vertumnus told Pomona a sad story of a young woman who had rejected a suitor. The young man was so distraught at the rejection that he killed himself. The young woman didn't care about the man or what he had done, so she was turned into a statue because of her hardened heart. Vertumnus (as the old woman) pleaded with Pomona to change her ways, lest she end up hardened like the young woman. At the end of the tale, Pomona wasn't moved to change her mind, so Vertumnus was forced to do something desperate. He shed the disguise of the old woman and exposed his real self to Pomona. She saw his handsome form and immediately fell madly in love with him. From then on, they looked after Pomona's garden together.

As the seasons change or when the apples ripen on the trees, remember the story of Vertumnus and Pomona. The mystery of Vertumnus is his power to transform himself into many forms, just as the growing garden changes from day to day.

THERE ARE SOME shrubs that seem to scream, "Look at me!" With their showy flowers and intense fragrance, planting just one of these shrubs can light up the whole yard. With so many exotic and unusual planting choices available, these common showstoppers are worth consideration.

Rhododendrons and the closely related azaleas are sure bets for a spectacular flower show. With large clusters of flowers in deep pink, yellow, purple, or white and their dark green foliage, these shrubs can surely be used alone or in groups to accent any yard. Both shrubs prefer a moist, shady growing area. There are some types of azaleas that can stand some direct sun, but rhododendrons do not survive well in intense light. Rhododendrons generally grow larger than azaleas—up to twenty feet tall compared with the smaller five-foot-tall azalea. Each plant has many different varieties to choose from, and the size and hardiness of the shrubs will vary with each variety.

Other shrubs with intense color, such as the hydrangea and forsythia, are commonly used as feature specimens in the yard. The hydrangea, growing four to eight feet tall (depending on the variety), has clusters of blooms up to a foot wide. While the flowers create a feast for the eyes, their color is dependent on the soil the shrub is planted in. When the soil for the hydrangea is acidic, the flowers blossom a deep blue. In alkaline soil, the flowers emerge colored from pink to red. Pruning is necessary to keep the bush in shape and encourage flower growth. The forsythia is one of the earliest blooming shrubs. The small, dramatic yellow flowers cling to the branches, often blooming before the foliage is out. These bushes need space to grow as they can reach six to ten feet high. They should be planted in full sun, and pruning should be done after the blooms are gone. The forsythia's dense branches make it easy to shape, creating an even more sensational show of color when in bloom.

Lilacs have the distinction of bringing both flowers and fragrance together to create a backyard attraction. The large clusters of tiny deep purple, lavender, pink, or white flowers offset beautiful, large green leaves, creating an instant bouquet on the branch. The intense scent of the lilacs will draw any passerby into its circle of sweet perfume. Lilacs thrive in full sun, reaching eight to fifteen feet high in maturity. While they will grow from Zones 3–7, lilacs are happiest in areas where winters are cold.

These types of shrubs may be considered commonplace, but they certainly are not ordinary. Their intensity makes one stop and take notice and perhaps feel compelled to give Mother Nature a round of applause for the fantastic show.

The old house rose before the Doctor, crowning a terraced garden, flanked at the left by an avenue of tall elms. The flower-beds were edged with box, which diffused around it that dreamy balsamic odor, full of ante-natal reminiscences of a lost Paradise, dimly fragrant as might be the bdellium of ancient Havilah, the land compassed by the river Pison that went out of Eden. The garden was somewhat neglected, but not in disgrace,—and in the time of tulips and hyacinths, of roses, of "snowballs," of honeysuckles, of lilacs, of syringas, it was rich with blossoms.

From the front-windows of the mansion the eye reached a far blue mountain-summit,—no rounded heap, such as often shuts in a village-landscape, but a sharp peak, clean-angled as Ascutney from the Dartmouth green. A wide gap through miles of woods had opened this distant view, and showed more, perhaps, than all the labors of the architect and the landscape-gardener the large style of the early Dudleys.

The great stone-chimney of the mansion-house was the centre from which all the artificial features of the scene appeared to flow. The roofs, the gables, the dormer-windows, the porches, the clustered offices in the rear, all seemed to crowd about the great chimney. To this central pillar the paths all converged. The single poplar behind the house—Nature is jealous of proud chimneys, and always loves to put a poplar near one, so that it may fling a leaf or two down its black throat every autumn—the one tall poplar behind the house seemed to nod and whisper to the grave square column, the elms to sway their branches towards it. And when the blue smoke rose from its summit, it seemed to be wafted away to join the azure haze which hung around the peak in the far distance, so that both should bathe in a common atmosphere.

Behind the house were clumps of lilacs with a century's growth upon them, and looking more like trees than like shrubs. Shaded by a group of these was the ancient well, of huge circuit, and with a low arch opening out of its wall about ten feet below the surface—whether the door of a crypt for the concealment of treasure, or of a subterranean passage, or merely of a vault for keeping provisions cool in hot weather, opinions differed.

Fragrant Box

FROM A LANDSCAPE maze to a hedgerow fashioned into a whimsical sea serpent, boxwood lends itself to all kinds of designs. Easy to care for and requiring little pruning, its dense growth makes perfect borders, providing years of hedging that is both lovely and practical. (Dwarf box, *Buxus sempervirens Suffruticosa*, is a dwarf form that only grows ½ an inch a year making it a perfect low edging plant.)

Boxwood is quite slow-growing and only reaches four to five feet at maturity. Boxwood can live for 100 years or longer and is a very low-maintenance shrub. Most varieties have small green, slightly glossy leaves, and their branches grow close together to form a perfect hedge. The Japanese, Korean, English, and American varieties all grow well in full sun or partial shade. They do best from Zones 6 to 9, through some more modern cultivars survive well into Zone 5.

Boxwood can be purchased from the nursery either in pots or bound in burlap, though potted plants are generally easier to handle. They should be spaced two to three feet apart in soil enhanced with compost. The plants need steady moisture and well-drained soil. Water them frequently throughout the first summer, spraying water on the foliage at the same time; mulch to retain moisture and retard weed growth. Fertilize carefully in the spring. Water the fertilizer into the ground instead of mixing it in around the plant; boxwoods have shallow roots, and the digging may irritate the root system. Prune in early spring to the desired shape. They grow so slowly, this annual pruning is all they'll require.

Boxwoods are marvelously fragrant, on warm summer days reminding one of ancient gardens and gravel crunching underfoot. While most find the scent delightful, a few disagree, so it's best to check out your scent preferences before purchase. Standard box (*Buxus sempervirens*) is the most fragrant of the group; modern cultivars have little or no smell at all.

As a hedge, topiary, or maze, the boxwood can be called the jack-of-all shrubs. Proper English gardens aren't complete without them, and many gardeners would think of nothing else to edge their precious landscapes. Plant boxwood, shape it any way you'd like, and enjoy it for many years to come.

OLIVER WENDELL HOLMES

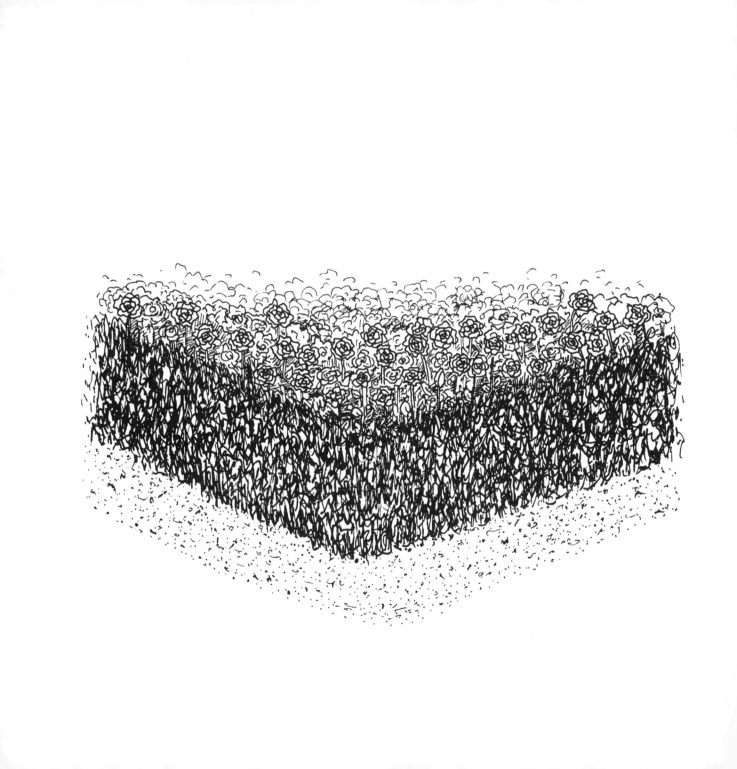

A Boxwood Nursery

IT'S EASY AND economical to start a boxwood nursery at home. Evergreen boxwoods, traditionally known for their formality, can be snipped and pruned into interesting shapes, small edgings, or tall hedges. Start by identifying a prime "parent" bush—say, a neighbor's or relative's lush specimen—and get the owner's permission to collect a small number of cuttings.

To prepare a site for a nursery, select a sheltered spot in the garden in spring or autumn. This area can be as large or as small as you like, though light shade is best. Add six to eight inches of topsoil and cover that with several inches of mulch. Soak the area heavily in the evening and again in the morning before planting. Or you can use a raised bed. To make one, nail four two-by-fours together to the size desired, and set them on the cultivated bed. Even a flat in a greenhouse or cold frame will do.

Clip cuttings of boxwood that are six to eight inches long. Strip any foliage from the lower two inches of the branch. Dip the base of the branch—from one to two inches—into Rootone®, a rooting hormone and fungicide readily available at garden centers.

Using an old screwdriver or other pointed object, punch a small hole in the soil. Pull the screwdriver out and gently push the cutting into the hole. Repeat with each cutting, planting them about 3 inches apart. Firm the soil up around the cuttings and water well to settle the soil. Keep evenly moist until the roots develop, usually in a month or so.

By the next spring or fall, the cuttings will be mature enough to be replanted in a permanent spot.

OLIVER WENDELL HOLMES

The Single Poplar

IN THE PAST, these fast-growing trees, closely related to the willow, lined many streets and driveways in America. Over time, however, the poplar's invasive root system put the tree out of favor in urban settings. The roots can break into drains and sewer systems and lift pavement, leading some communities to ban all varieties, even though it was only one species, the Carolina poplar, that was the primary culprit. This is a shame because under the right circumstances, the poplar makes an excellent addition to the landscape.

Both the white and Japanese poplars have much to recommend them. White or bolleana poplars have beautiful gray green leaves with powdery white undersides. The slightest breeze will cause the leaves to turn over and display their shimmery white bottoms giving the appearance of a thousand miniature fans aflutter. The Japanese poplar features coarse green leaves that unfold very early in the spring: here it's the tree's light-colored bark that makes it so effective in landscape.

Poplars can grow a foot or more a year, to a height of up to seventy feet. They make excellent if somewhat short-lived screens. They can survive in just about any soil and need little, if any, tending. Carefully plan the placement of the tree, as its roots can grow a bit wild and the wood is weak; branches can likely break off in a heavy wind or snowstorm. Plant the tree off by itself and watch it grow steadily year after year, a lively exclamation point in any landscape.

There was a stone seat in a corner, one or two mouldy statues, some trellises loosened by time and rotting upon the wall; no walks, moreover, nor turf; dog-grass everywhere. Horticulture had departed and nature had returned. Weeds were abundant, a wonderful hap for a poor bit of earth. The heyday of the gilliflowers was splendid. Nothing in this garden opposed the sacred effort of things towards life; venerable growth was at home there. The trees bent over towards the briers, the briers mounted towards the trees, the shrub had climbed, the branch had bowed, that which runs upon the ground had attempted to find that which blooms in the air, that which floats in the wind had stooped towards that which trails in the moss; trunks, branches, leaves, twigs, tufts, tendrils, shoots, thorns, were mingled, crossed, married, confounded; vegetation, in a close and strong embrace, had celebrated and accomplished there under the satisfied eye of the Creator, in this inclosure of three hundred feet square, the sacred mystery of its fraternity, symbol of human fraternity. This garden was no longer a garden; it was a colossal bush, that is to say, something which is as impenetrable as a forest, populous as a city, tremulous as a nest, dark as a cathedral, odorous as a bouquet, solitary as a tomb, full of life as a multitude.

The Garden Gone Wild

A CRUMBLED WALL in a neglected garden gone wild should be repaired, right? Not necessarily. Take a closer look and discover the many wonderful and colorful plants that have made the nooks and crannies of this broken structure their home. This setting and its inhabitants can be as intriguing as any intended ornamentation in the garden.

Usually, the first things to take over the toppled rocks are moss and lichen, which provide that green, wild look. This may appear a sign of neglect, but nature is just providing a lovely background for other plants to grow. Ferns, such as the hart's tongue and common polypody, grow and drape themselves over the rocks for dramatic effect. Hens and chicks, not only charming because of the name, are rosettes of green and red leaves that produce pink, red, and purple flowers. They grow from the cracks and crevices, multiplying madly to form dense clusters of color. Other plants that can establish themselves in this wild setting are common rockroses, which are sun-loving bushy plants that grow no more than a foot high. The flowers bloom in white, pink, red, and yellow, and grow proudly from the dark-green foliage. Sedum, with its variety of colored leaf clusters, also give color with white, yellow, and purple flowers.

None of these plants asks for much in the way of soil, water, or other attention. They not only survive in this setting, they thrive in it. Instead of seeing these wild creatures as garden squatters that need evicting, think about keeping them and working around them in their makeshift home. Better yet, purposely plant these hardy blokes in the nooks of your garden and bring a little wildness to your life. In any case, remember that the wealth of plant life that can grow on its own on an old, crumbled wall or other neglected corners of your garden is worth examining, for nature's own random input is often more interesting than anything the gardener can plan.

VICTOR HUGO

The Heyday of the Gillyflowers

LONG AGO, THE Normans brought the gillyflower to England, where it was prized for its spicy fragrance and striking beauty. This hardy bloomer was widely naturalized and found its way into many drawings of medieval times. Because gillyflowers prospered in harsh climates and conditions, they became known as symbols of faithfulness in adversity. Needless to say, gillyflowers can be cultivated in any climate zone.

Also known as *Matthiola incana*, queen stock, and brampton stock, the gillyflower has been hybridized into many different types. Flowers can be single- or double-bloomers with blossoms of red, pink, purple, blue, yellow, or white. While most strains are annuals, if happy with their site, most gillyflowers will self-seed, providing years of fragrant bloom.

Gillyflowers are often used in borders and cutting gardens and can be grown in pots. Stems reaching up to two and a half feet bear flower clusters in summer, fall, and winter, depending on your climate and planting time. They make excellent cut flowers.

Gillyflowers may be propagated by taking cuttings from mature plants. However, plants raised from seed are stronger and produce large, healthy flowers. Seeds should be sown in late spring. Gillyflowers enjoy rich, well-drained soil in full sun. Mature plants and seed are available from local garden centers or through mail-order catalogs.

Sons and Lovers

She became aware of something about her. With an effort she roused herself to see what it was that penetrated her consciousness. The tall white lilies were reeling in the moonlight, and the air was charged with their perfume, as with a presence. Mrs. Morel gasped slightly in fear. She touched the big, pallid flowers on their petals, then shivered. They seemed to be stretching in the moonlight. She put her hand into one white bin: the gold scarcely showed on her fingers by moonlight. She bent down to look at the binful of yellow pollen; but it only appeared dusky. Then she drank a deep draught of the scent. It almost made her dizzy.

Mrs. Morel leaned on the garden gate, looking out, and she lost herself awhile. She did not know what she thought. Except for a slight feeling of sickness, and her consciousness in the child, herself melted out like scent into the shiny, pale air. After a time the child, too, melted with her in the mixing-pot of moonlight, and she rested with the hills and lilies and houses, all swum together in a kind of swoon.

When she came to herself she was tired for sleep. Languidly she looked about her; the clumps of white phlox seemed like bushes spread with linen; a moth ricocheted over them, and right across the garden. Following it with her eye roused her. A few whiffs of the raw, strong scent of phlox invigorated her. She passed along the path, hesitating at the white rose-bush. It smelled sweet and simple. She touched the white ruffles of the roses. Their fresh scent and cool, soft leaves reminded her of the morning-time and sunshine. She was very fond of them. But she was tired, and wanted to sleep. In the mysterious out-of-doors she felt forlorn.

THE LILY IS an ideal, showy perennial that should find a home in every garden. Regarded as the oldest cultivated flower, lilies send up spires of majestic blooms in a dazzling array of colors throughout the summer growing season. There is a broad range to choose from; plants can be selected by desired height, flower color and form, blossom season, and growing requirements. Colors include white, yellow, pink, red, orange, and spotted. Lilies are long-lived and produce a profusion of blooms, year after year.

Lily bulbs can be purchased in the spring and fall and should be planted immediately since they are never dormant. Plant bulbs six inches deep in well-drained soil in half- or full-day sun. Many will thrive in shade. Keep in mind that a lily plant in bloom will spread nine to fifteen inches, so it is important when planting a large stand—which will have spectacular effect—not to plant the bulbs too close, or the plant may have fewer blossoms because of a lack of space. Lilies can also be grown in pots. That way, they can be moved about as necessary—either as filler or placed nearby for special enjoyment at peak blooming times. Many varieties are extremely fragrant.

The soil should be prepared thoroughly. Remove any weeds and loosen and rake the soil. Cover the planting area with a one-inch blanket of organic matter: manure, leaf mold, compost, sawdust, and/or lawn clippings. Next, make sure the water is draining properly. If not, mix builder's sand with the planting soil to loosen it. Next, work a small handful of bone meal into the planting soil. It is one of the best natural fertilizers readily available: rich in phosphorus, it aids in developing strong and healthy root systems. When all the soil amendments have been added, work them into the soil with a pitchfork or rotary tilling machine, which can be rented from a local equipment rental center. Tilling will create air spaces in the soil, allowing water and nutrients to pass through and nourish the roots.

Staking should be done just before blooming, when the plant has reached one-half to two-thirds of its projected height. Place a garden stake 18 inches from the stem to prevent the bulb from being punctured. The lily will reach its full height in the second year.

D. H. LAWRENCE

Lilies will bloom from four to six weeks, some beginning as early as June. Successive flowering is achieved by careful planning and selection. Some mail-order garden catalogs list species chronologically in order of bloom time, making the selection task that much easier.

Cultivation is rarely necessary when the bulbs are planted correctly, but overcrowding is a common problem. Simply dig up the plants, divide, and replant at a new site. It may take a season for the small plants to become established and begin to bloom prolifically.

Lilies are prone to several pests and diseases: If one appears, deal with it right away. Viral symptoms include mottled or twisted leaves; discard these plants as soon as possible. Likewise, discard any plants that show signs of gray mold, and spray healthy plants with a fungicide. Cut leaves may be a sign of red lily beetles. Pick them off by hand and spray the plant with insecticidal soap.

Fertilize lily plants in the spring with a dusting of 5-10-5 fertilizer. Lily bulbs multiply each year. Division will become necessary in one or two years when the plant produces fewer flowers. Another more cost-effective but tedious and time-consuming method of propagation is to sow lily seeds in pots of commercial soilless potting mix. Cover with a layer of gravel and store in a cool place with minimal light.

Lilies can be generally grouped into different categories according to bloom time, form, height, and size: trumpets, Asiatic, Oriental hybrids, martagon, unclassified hybrids, and species types.

Trumpets (like the famous Easter lily) reach heights of up to eight feet tall, are exceptionally fragrant, and grow best in moderate winter climates. The Asiatic is the earliest bloomer, known to flower as early as May and continuing through the end of June. The exquisite blooms are upfacing but not fragrant. It multiplies very quickly and is extremely easy to care for. The Orientals produce the most elegant and refined blossoms of all the lily species. The converging stalks are a piece of art in themselves. These charmers require little care in areas where average daytime temperatures stay below eighty-five degrees, and they are very prolific bloomers.

A small sea of lilies makes a spectacular statement in the garden. Watch them reel in the moonlight, or just take time to stroke their luscious, smooth petals.

A Tapestry of White Phlox

CHARMING AND LOYAL, summer phlox lends an elegant air to the garden and dutifully carries the flower borders from one blooming season into the next. Its colorful clouds of spice-scented blossoms burst at the tips of tall, slender stalks. Phlox's free-blooming ways make it indispensable to the flower gardener.

When the garden and gardener begin to fade in summer's wearying heat, phlox carries the day. Tiny flowerets cluster in conical shapes about ten to fourteen inches across, creating lavish displays of blossoms from July to August in colors ranging from red, pink, and salmon to purple, lavender, and white.

Phlox may be grown from seed. However, this is a long, tedious process; it can take one to three years to produce a flowering plant. Phlox is best grown from nursery plants or by division. This way, the plants produce flowers much more quickly.

Plant this lovely stalwart in deep, moist, well-drained soil rich in organic matter and superphosphate. Choose a planting site in full sun. If necessary, the phlox will tolerate slight shade. Water the plants early in the day to prevent powdery mildew, the bane of phlox. The warmth of the sun will dry the foliage and help prevent the problem. Keep them well-watered during droughts. Fertilize regularly in spring and early summer and clip spent flower heads just below the last flower to encourage more blooms.

D. H. LAWRENCE

The Big Stand of Madonna Lilies

THE WHITE MADONNA lily reigns supreme in the garden, where its blooms take their throne in June or July. The Madonna lily has its roots in biblical times; even then it was known for its heavy fragrance and purity of color.

Known botanically as *L. candidum*, the Madonna lily grows up to four feet high and prefers a sunny spot. Bulbs can be planted in the fall or spring in well-drained soil with plenty of organic matter. The bulb should be planted an inch deep (a planting preference unique among the lilies). Position the lily so the top stems are able to reach toward the warmth of the midday sun, and allow other plants to shade the roots.

The Madonna lily can also be planted in pots and set along a garden path or moved elsewhere to create a stunning focal point. Gray foliage and pink flowering plants make suitable companions and create a pleasing effect in the garden. The Madonna lily has a greater tolerance than other lilies for alkaline soil and summer heat; in fact, it actually prefers the addition of a little lime. Hardy to Zone 4, this gem of a lily has been known to luxuriate in an array of growing conditions from hot and dry to damp, moist, and shady nooks.

"Bliss"

The windows of the drawing-room opened on to a balcony overlooking the garden. At the far end, against the wall, there was a tall, slender pear tree in fullest, richest bloom; it stood perfect, as though becalmed against the jade-green sky. Bertha couldn't help feeling, even from this distance, that it had not a single bud or a faded petal. Down below, in the garden beds, the red and yellow tulips, heavy with flowers, seemed to lean upon the dusk. A grey cat, dragging its belly, crept across the lawn, and a black one, its shadow, trailed after. The sight of them, so intent and so quick, gave Bertha a curious shiver.

"What creepy things cats are!" she stammered, and she turned away from the window and began walking up and down. . . .

How strong the jonquils smelled in the warm room. Too strong? Oh, no. And yet, as though overcome, she flung down on a couch and pressed her hands to her eyes.

"I'm too happy—too happy!" she murmured.

And she seemed to see on her eyelids the lovely pear tree with its wide open blossoms as a symbol of her own life.

A Lovely Pear Tree

NATIVE TO ASIA and Eastern Europe, the pear (*pyrus communis*) has been an important food crop since prehistoric times. Several named varieties were known to the Ancient Greeks as early as 370 B.C., and the Romans prized the fruit so much that they carried it to the far corners of their empire. Arriving in America with the first colonists, the pear has continued to be a favorite in the garden ever since.

Pears are fairly easy to grow, if you keep a few important facts in mind. The pear tree grows best in a warm, sheltered, sunny site with well-drained soil. Flowering in mid- to late spring, most pears are not fully self-fertile and need at least one other variety planted close by for pollination to set fruit. Even trees labeled self-fertile perform better when they are cross-fertilized by another variety. Don't expect the tree to fruit the first year: It may take as long as three or four years for a tree to bear a good crop, but once it does it will continue producing for decades.

Pears can be planted in the spring, but even better is to plant pear trees in the fall while the soil is still warm so the tree can establish itself before new spring growth. Check the tree's label to ensure adequate planting distances. Routine care includes keeping the tree well watered in dry spells, occasionally applying fertilizer and pruning. In early summer after "June drop" (when the tree naturally sheds imperfect and diseased fruit), thin the remaining fruits to improve the size, quality and flavor, and to prevent any branches from breaking.

The pear's growing season stretches from spring through the first frost. The fruit is ready for harvest when the stems separate easily from the tree. Pick the pears—keeping the stem on the fruit—slightly before they ripen from their dark green color to a light yellow. Early and late ripening varieties are available. The early varieties should be eaten right away; later varieties are perfect for winter storage when wrapped in tissue paper and placed in a cool, dry area.

Like most other fruit trees, pears are prey to a variety of diseases and pests. Some pests to look out for include the codling moth, San Jose scale, and pear slugs; diseases include fire blight, canker, and powdery mildew. Spraying may be required if you want perfect, unblemished fruit.

If you've inherited a neglected old pear tree, get out your pruning shears and follow these easy directions for a pruning renewal: Prune the tree to a manageable height, approximately fifteen to twenty feet, and remove all dead, diseased, and damaged branches. Next, eliminate the weak, crisscrossing branches and cut off any suckers.

It is best to use a major limb as a central leader. If there isn't one, prune the top into an open fan shape to let in light and air. Add compost, rotted manure or 10-10-10 fertilizer underneath the drip line of the tree. Then add a top layer of mulch and water generously.

There are a variety of pear trees to choose from depending on the kind of fruit you're looking for and where you live. Some of the hardier varieties include Beurre Giffard, Beurre Hardy, Golden Spice and Lincoln. Seckel is another favorite of home gardeners. Its small, firm, sweet fruit is good for eating off the tree or for making spiced or pickled pears. Chopin is a tasty early pear. The fruit is smooth and sweet and the plant compact. Bartlett pears are known for their juicy, sweet flavor and are excellent for canning and commercial production. Beurre Bose is a good pear for eating off the tree. Its fruit is slower to ripen, but worth waiting for.

❧ *The Cat in the Garden* ❧

FROM PATIO PLANTERS to acres of farmland, cats the world over are keeping a watchful eye on plants. Why do they make such good garden mascots? Here are five reasons why having a cat in the garden is reason enough to have a cat.

1. They can help plan and plant a garden. A cat can spot the most delectable and tender plants. Just give him a few leaves to inspect, and he'll make his preferences known. Let him also select the perfect spot for catnip, his afternoon snack. Cats are fun planting companions. Their busy paws will tamp down the soil, keeping tiny seeds safe. And his playful scratching will unearth dry spots that need to be watered.

2. Cats are also natural pollinators. Like bees, they transport pollen from plant to plant. But unlike the flying insects, cats rub up against anything their little hearts desire. As they lovingly caress plants with their whiskers and faces, they collect pollen to deposit at the next object of affection. Cats have long been known to mark their territories with this rubbing habit, but little did anyone know they had a secret desire to make the garden grow.

3. Rodent control is the perennial concern for the gardener. Instead of investing scads of money in rodent control, get a cat. Everyone knows that cats take care of mice, but a less-

er-known animosity exists between cats and gophers and moles. Cats naturally discourage moles from munching on tulip bulbs or a pesky rabbit from devouring the lettuce.

4. Gardens need to be weeded, pruned, and generally tended. Cats are habitual weeders and pruners. Those tiny blades of grass that plague every row of every vegetable garden are especially attractive to cats. They chew them up before the strands can lose their tender shoots to a trusty rake. Then there's the free fertilizer cats provide. Burying their donations aerates the soil and helps the ground soak up precious nutrients.

5. Finally, ornamentation is a goal of many gardeners. Many feel the need to supplement nature's splendor with ornaments of their own. Hand-painted signs mark garden rows. Stone frogs and gargoyles poise at the garden's edge, while colorful windsocks dance on a nearby shed. Cats are the great unsung—and animated—garden ornament. The vain feline will choose places to sit that highlight his natural beauty; a cat will never rest where it is unflattering. Nothing on the shelves of the garden store compares with the decorative presence of a cat.

So keep an open mind when it comes to having a cat in the garden. That feline lazing in the sunshine amid the hardy mums is just there to help.

KATHERINE MANSFIELD

The Scarlet Pimpernel

She looked at Sir Andrew with eager curiosity. The young man's face had become almost transfigured. His eyes shone with enthusiasm; hero-worship, love, admiration for his leader seemed literally to glow upon his face. "The Scarlet Pimpernel, Mademoiselle," he said at last, "is the name of a humble English wayside flower; but it is also the name chosen to hide the identity of the best and bravest man in all the world, so that he may better succeed in accomplishing the noble task he has set himself to do."

The Scarlet Pimpernel

SCARLET PIMPERNEL IS the common name for a humble English wayside flower. *Anagallis arvensis*, as it is known botanically, is a four-inch-high plant that creeps unceremoniously across field and furrow. Single red blooms are borne atop delicate stems (occasionally blue or white flowers are also found). The blossoms are upward-facing and close up each day in midafternoon or with the onset of clouds, earning it the nickname "poor man's weatherglass."

The pimpernel is not readily available in the United States. However, if you can locate seeds or a root cutting, the pimpernel is easy to grow and care for when planted in well-drained, dry soil in full sun. Propagation is brought about from seed, cuttings, or root division. While an annual, it readily self-sows. Seeds should be planted in fall or spring in a spot where the plant can stay, since it is difficult to transplant.

In Europe this wildflower grows in sandy soil along roadsides, fields, and lawns requiring little or no care.

Once considered an herb, scarlet pimpernel was said to be a medical cure-all and a mental stimulant. However, the plant can be poisonous and should be only used for its old-fashioned ornamental value.

BARONESS EMMUSKA ORCZY

Remembrance of Things Past: Swann's Way

I found the whole path throbbing with the fragrance of hawthorn-blossom. The hedge resembled a series of chapels, whose walls were no longer visible under the mountains of flowers that were heaped upon their altars; while beneath them the sun cast a checkered light upon the ground, as though I had been standing before the Lady-altar, and the flowers, themselves adorned also, held out each its little bunch of glittering stamens with an absentminded air, delicate radiating veins in the flamboyant style like those which, in the church, framed the stairway to the rood-loft or the mullions of the windows and blossomed out into the fleshy whiteness of strawberry-flowers. How simple and rustic by comparison would seem the dog-roses which in a few weeks' time would be climbing the same path in the heat of the sun, dressed in the smooth silk of their blushing pink bodices that dissolve in the first breath of wind.

HAWTHORNS, ALSO KNOWN as thorn apples, are attractive flowering shrubs that when planted in rows make excellent borders. They are lovely year-round plants with white/pink flowers in spring, bright red fruit in the summer, leaves that turn orange red in fall, and interlocking branches that provide a wonderful background to winter snow. Native to eastern North America, there are hundreds of varieties of hawthorns in the country, though only 20 or so are of interst in the landscape. Among these are the Cockspur hawthorn and the Washington hawthorn.

The cockspur hawthorn is a bush or small tree that can grow up to 30 feet high. With its horizontal branches and two-inch thorns, it creates a ready-made partition when planted as a hedgerow. The clusters of white, fragrant flowers appear in May to June against dark green foliage. After flowering, glossy red fruit resembling miniature apples appears. The fruit will stay on the tree well into the fall, if the birds don't get it first. The leaves turn beautiful autumn colors and fall off to reveal the web of branches and thorns in winter. The Washington hawthorn is virtually identical to the cockspur in appearance and manner, but the foliage is glossier and the berries more prominent. It is also one of the latest hawthorns to bloom and endures urban conditions well.

For hedges, hawthorns should be planted three to four feet apart to allow the branches room to mesh together. When planted, cut back the bush by one-half, and mulch and fertilize to advance growth. Allow the plant a year to get

MARCEL PROUST

established before pruning, which should be done in late February or early March before the weather warms. Always prune with the thorns in mind, both for personal safety and for the safety of any passer-by to the hedgerow. Unfortunately, one drawback to hawthorns is their susceptibility to a wide variety of pests and diseases, especially fire blight. Treat any problem swiftly to prevent spreading. Both varieties are hardy from Zones 4 to 8, and should be planted in well-drained soil in full sun for best results.

The hawthorn is a dramatic addition to any landscape; it's sturdy, purposeful, and good-looking, and its changing appearance throughout the year makes it seem like four plants in one; for any frugal gardener, this is a match made in heaven.

Garden Memories

VIVID MEMORIES OF childhood continue to live in our mind's eye: trees just perfect for climbing, tea parties hosted in shady garden nooks, scented magnolia blossoms, brittle autumn leaves crunching underfoot, the pungent aroma of pine. Plants can help rekindle those memories.

Scent triggers powerful pictures. A basket of freshly cut jasmine, a fistful of daffodils, and the fragrance of sweet gardenias may recall a grandmother's front porch. Through christenings, graduations, and weddings, scented memories continue to flow through the years of people's lives.

Mixing memory-evoking scents and scenes into the gardens of today also helps create memories for today's children. It could be something as enterprising as building a tree house or planting a delicate miniature rosebush laden with pink blossoms in summer. Or it could be as simple as providing strawberries to be plucked and flowers to be picked for a child's bouquet.

Consider these possibilities:

- Building a birdhouse that resembles the church where your parents were married or your childhood home
- Planting a stand of sunflowers for a natural children's playhouse
- Playing hide and seek in a planting of tasseled cornstalks
- Picking brightly colored zinnias grown in a thicket
- Chasing fireflies on a summer night

With a little imagination and a bit of elbow grease, you can create a whole wealth of remembrances of things past right in your own garden.

MARCEL PROUST

Rootabaga Stories:
"How to Tell Corn Fairies If You See 'Em"

If you have ever watched the little corn begin to march across the black lands and then slowly change to big corn and go marching on from the little corn moon of summer to the big corn harvest moon of autumn, then you must have guessed who it is that helps the corn come along. It is the corn fairies. Leave out the corn fairies and there wouldn't be any corn.

All children know this. All boys and girls know that corn is no good unless there are corn fairies.

Have you ever stood in Illinois or Iowa and watched the late summer wind or the early fall wind running across a big cornfield? It looks as if a big, long blanket were being spread out for dancers to come and dance on. If you look close and if you listen close you can see the corn fairies come dancing and singing—sometimes. If it is a wild day and a hot sun is pouring down while a cool north wind blows—and this happens sometimes—then you will be sure to see thousands of corn fairies marching and countermarching in mocking grand marches over the big, long blanket of green and silver. Then too they sing, only you must listen with your littlest and newest ears if you wish to hear their singing. They sing soft songs that go pla-sizzy pla-sizzy-sizzy, and each song is softer than an eye wink, softer than a Nebraska baby's thumb.

And Spink, who is a little girl living in the same house with the man writing this story, and Skabootch, who is another little girl in the same house—both Spink and Skabootch are asking the question, "How can we tell corn fairies if we see 'em? If we meet a corn fairy how will we know it?" And this is the explanation the man gave to Spink who is older than Skabootch, and to Skabootch who is younger than Spink:—

All corn fairies wear overalls. They work hard, the corn fairies, and they are proud. The reason they are proud is because they work so hard. And the reason they work so hard is because they have overalls.

But understand this. The overalls are corn gold cloth, woven from leaves of ripe corn mixed with ripe October corn silk. In the first week of the harvest moon coming up red and changing to yellow and silver the corn fairies sit by thousands between the corn rows weaving and stitching the clothes they have to wear next winter, next spring, next summer.

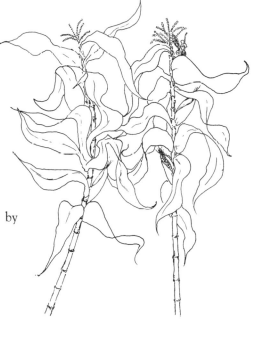

The Corn Fairies' Dance

MAIZE HAS BEEN planted, eaten, worshiped, processed, and profited from for centuries. It was the main cereal of the New World and supported early civilizations of the Americas. It was even the salvation of the pilgrims: Squanto taught the pilgrims how to cultivate and use maize, enabling them to survive in the New World.

Corn, as maize is commonly known today, is a fun and easy crop to grow, especially with children. Aside from the summertime delight of rolling slippery yellow cobs in bars of soft butter, the tall stalks make amusing settings for games of hide-and-seek and pretend.

Corn will tolerate most soil conditions but prefers a deep, well-manured plot. Native Americans put a dead fish into the soil with every kernel for fertilizer. Unless fish are in plentiful supply in your area, turn the soil over and add a layer of compost and 10-10-10 fertilizer (approximately five pounds to one hundred square feet) and mix in thoroughly.

The actual planting is simple. In spring, after the last frost and when the ground has warmed, plant a couple of kernels together one inch deep and twelve inches apart in blocks at least four rows wide. Corn is pollinated by the wind and should be planted in groups instead of one continuous row. When the tassels appear, apply fish emulsion, a liquid fertilizer or granular 10-10-10. To provide for a continuous supply of corn, plant successive crops every ten to fourteen days through midsummer or until about ninety days before the first frost. Time the plantings to ensure that at least ten days elapse between pollination periods. Corn grows rapidly in warm weather. It becomes important to keep the plants well watered as the crop matures—from tasseling time to picking time. If the leaves begin to fold, check the soil for moisture.

Harvest the corn when the silks have turned completely brown. The ears should appear full in size and be firm to the touch. You can always check by pulling the husk back and taking a peek. To pick the ears, hold the stalk firmly and snap the ear downward and then up. The corn should be used as soon as possible, since it begins to turn starchy within hours. After the harvest, pull up and discard the dry cornstalks. Add more manure and fertilizer and replant with corn seedlings. This continuous planting method will provide fresh corn for the dinner table through September or October. Children will also enjoy bundling the dried cornstalks and using them along with pumpkins and squash to make autumn decorations.

Beware of the corn borer. This pest can be treated with the insecticide Sevin, but be sure to read the instructions carefully before use. Biological controls are also available. Other common pests include birds and squirrels. As soon as the corn has been pollinated, the ears can be protected by putting a paper bag over each ear of corn in the garden. If a plot of land is not available, corn can easily be grown in containers on a patio or balcony. It is important to use a soilless mix to prevent water from escaping too quickly, a common malady of container-grown plants.

Any seed corn variety will do. Simply follow the planting instructions listed above. An underplanting of lettuce works nicely to keep the soil moist. When selecting seed corn varieties, consider zone, days to maturation, ear length, rows per ear, and stalk height to assure a satisfying harvest. Special varieties include:

Extra early: Super Sweet, Early Sweet Hybrid, Buttervee
Early: Spring Gold, Sprite
Midseason: Butter and Sugar, Tastynee
Main: Seneca Chief
Wonderful late: Silver Queen, Sweet Sue

And be sure to keep your eyes out for corn fairies.

Corn Relish

FRESH CORN MEANS sweet, juicy kernels that are full of flavor. Preserving the fresh taste of corn is essential after all the hard work of growing it. Many home corn growers have the water boiling even before they go out to pick. Ears of corn can be shucked and cooked whole or the kernels cut off and used in recipes. Grilling corn in the husk creates a unique smoky flavor perfect for an outdoor barbecue. For those who don't grow their own, fresh corn is widely available at roadside stands and in the supermarket. To choose the best ears, first look at the bottom of the husk to see if it's really fresh. The bottom portion that has been cut from the stalk should be relatively moist and not dried out and brown. Then, peel back part of the husk and look at the kernels. They should be plump and firm. Use fresh corn as soon as possible because the longer it sits after picking, the less sweet and more starchy it will become. When fresh corn isn't available for use in recipes, frozen corn is a fine substitute; just thaw it in the refrigerator. To freeze your freshly picked corn, blanch it on the cob for one to two minutes in boiling water, cool, then freeze whole or cut the kernels off and freeze them in well-sealed plastic bags.

2 tablespoons olive oil

1 cup corn kernels

1 red bell pepper, finely diced

1 green bell pepper, finely diced

2 tablespoons red onion, finely diced

1½ tablespoons balsamic vinegar

1½ tablespoons coarsely chopped cilantro

½ jalapeño pepper, seeded and minced

Salt and pepper, to taste

Heat 1 tablespoon olive oil in a heavy skillet and sauté corn kernels for one to two minutes, until slightly brown. Combine corn with other ingredients and remaining olive oil and season to taste with salt and pepper. Refrigerate for an hour to combine flavors. Can be served cold or at room temperature.

YIELD: About 2 cups

 Cornhusk Dolls

NATIVE AMERICAN TRIBES have used cornhusks for centuries to make baskets, masks, mats, and cornhusk dolls. Anyone can make these traditional dolls by using husks shucked from the corn for dinner. With few materials and a little time, this part of the corn can last well after the last ear is eaten.

The cornhusks used for making the dolls can be fresh or dried. If using fresh, carefully pull the husks from the ear, trying to keep as many whole and as long as possible. To make this easier, cut around the bottom of the ear with a sharp knife, slicing through the husk layers to the corn. Peel the husks from around the corn, starting from the bottom. The husks may be used immediately or dried for later use. To dry, lay the husks in a single layer (if they overlap too much, they may mold) in a well-ventilated area and leave for two to three days. Store them in a paper bag until ready to use. Soak the dried husks in warm water for five minutes to make them pliable when shaping the dolls.

To make the dolls, gather some string, a few cotton balls, and the cornhusks. Lay the cotton balls in the middle of a long husk, fold it over, and tie it under the cotton with string to shape the head. Roll two husks together and tie with string an inch from each end to form the arms and hands. Slip the arms under the head, then secure with string under the arms to make the waist. Circle the doll with six to ten lengthwise cornhusks, covering up the body. Tie these securely around the middle. Fold the husks down in half from the top to form the bottom of the doll. Leave as is for a skirt, or separate the husks into two sections and tie at the bottom for feet. Dry the dolls for a day or two, then decorate them with markers, paint, or fabric, and glue on some yarn or corn silk for hair.

Preserving the tradition of making cornhusk dolls is as simple as shucking an ear of corn. And while the custom may not last in your family for centuries, it will keep the kids busy after dinner.

Uncle Tom's Cabin

The cabin of Uncle Tom was a small log building, close adjoining to "the house," as the negro par excellence designates his master's dwelling. In front it had a neat garden-patch, where, every summer, strawberries, raspberries, and a variety of fruits and vegetables, flourished under careful tending. The whole front of it was covered by a large scarlet begonia and a native multiflora rose, which, entwisting and interlacing, left scarce a vestige of the rough logs to be seen. Here, also, in summer, various brilliant annuals, such as marigolds, petunias, four-o'clocks, found an indulgent corner in which to unfold their splendors, and were the delight and pride of Aunt Chloe's heart.

❧ An Indulgent Corner of Annuals ❧

FOR A GARDEN OF compelling color, indulge in a collection of brilliant annuals. These easy-to-care-for plants will quickly transform a garden into a flowering tapestry. They bloom from early summer until the first frost in autumn. Their entire life cycle takes place in one growing season: The plant germinates, flowers, sets seed, and dies. Because they won't be wintering over, annuals can be grown in any zone.

In colder climates, an annual is considered to be any plant that won't winter over in the garden. Popular varieties include the tall, heat-loving four-o'clocks, hardy petunias, sunny marigolds, zinnias, dense-headed ageratum, geraniums, snowy baby's breath, shade-loving impatiens, quick-climbing morning glory, and self-sowing nasturtium. The varieties are endless. Annuals will ramble over fences, climb walls, grow in compact mounds, and festoon containers of any size or shape, enriching the garden with their scent, foliage, bloom, and texture. As an added bonus, some varieties will happily self-sow for the next growing season. These plants are an ideal choice for quick coverage and are excellent for experimenting with new garden designs from year to year.

When selecting annuals, consider color, needs, habits, flower shape, foliage height, and texture. Combine different forms and colors or mass single varieties together for a dazzling effect. There are four different height categories: low, small, medium, and tall. The plants should be grouped so that the tall plants will not shade or cover the smaller varieties.

Consult the growing instructions to make sure the plants are placed appropriately. When coordinating colors, use the artist's color wheel to simplify the task. For a smooth, harmonious effect, select colors that are near each other on the color wheel, such as green, blue green, and blue. For striking impact, use contrasting colors—colors opposite each other on the color wheel—like orange and blue or red and green.

Still uncertain where to begin? Just visit a garden center. Make a list of what you like and ask the experts what works well in your area. Be sure to read the labels so your selection includes a variety of heights. Annuals can be purchased as seeds or as starter plants. Farmers' markets are a wonderful

KEY

IMPATIEN
PETUNIA
MARIGOLD
FOUR O'CLOCK
GERANIUM
NASTURTIUM
ZINNIA
BABY'S BREATH
AGERATUM
MORNING GLORY

An Indulgent Corner

source of interesting and hardy varieties at good prices, and the farmers generally love to give advice. Seed catalog companies and garden centers also sell prepackaged collections with different themes in mind. This makes it easy for the beginner or weekend gardener. Some annual collections, for instance, are designed to attract butterflies and hummingbirds or offer blooms in the same color palette. Others collect plants that thrive in shaded recesses or sunlit corners or that are everlasting and can be dried for later use in the home or for crafts. Heirloom collections are also popular. These packages come complete with seeds, markers, planting designs, and planting instructions. It's a great way to begin.

As with all gardening endeavors, it is of utmost importance to prepare the soil. In the fall, turn over the soil in new flower beds and dig deeply. Add organic matter and, if the soil is especially heavy, mix in sand. Make sure the soil drains well. If drainage becomes a problem, dig a trench at the edge of the garden and shovel the soil into the bed to raise the ground level. If adding annuals to cover bulbs, it won't be necessary to prepare the soil—it should already be in good condition.

Don't sow or plant annuals until after the last expected frost date in your area. Annuals added to the garden ahead of time will simply freeze. Throughout the season, keep the plants watered but not soaking wet. Don't depend on summer rainfall. Mulch to protect the roots and prevent weed growth; a layer of shredded hardwood mulch also adds to the garden's attractiveness. Once a month during the growing season, add a slow-release fertilizer.

Annuals aren't picky; they will thrive in containers, in borders along flower beds and garden walks, in hanging pots, in freestanding island gardens, or mixed in with perennials or vegetables. Wherever they grow, their blooms will bring brilliant, heartwarming splendor to any garden.

Raspberries

RASPBERRIES ARE ONE of the easiest fruits to grow. The sweet, colorful berries make it well worth planting a bush or two. Raspberry bushes are generally divided among four categories according to the berry color—red, yellow, purple, and black. Different colors are suited to different climate zones.

The red and yellow types are closely related and are divided into two groups: those that only fruit once a year, and others called "ever-bearing," which fruit in early summer and again in September until the first frost. While the ever-bearing types produce more fruit, the quality and size of the berries arc not as good as the single crop types, so for best yields, be sure to include bushes from both groups. All grow well in colder climates, from Zones 3 to 6. The single-crop red varieties include Canby, with large, bright-red berries and branches that are practically free from thorns, and Lantham, which is a hardy bush with good fruit for canning and freezing. Indian Summer and September are good ever-bearing reds. Yellow raspberries, such as Golden Mayberry, are very sweet. This type of raspberry bush is a very early type, with blooms beginning as early as April and fruit-bearing by June. Fallgolden is another good yellow ever-bearing choice. The purple varieties, like Sodus and Brandywine, have deep-purple berries that grow better in warmer climates. The black raspberry, like Cumberland, is prized for making jam and is also better suited to warmer areas.

Plant raspberries in the spring in a sunny location with good drainage. The soil for raspberries should be prepared with compost or grass clippings to a depth of six inches. Plant them where they can remain undisturbed, as these bushes will happily produce for fifteen years or more. Place the plants two to three feet apart in rows. The bushes should be planted in a one-foot-diameter hole with the base at ground level. Spread the roots out, put remaining soil back in, and water immediately to prevent air pockets. Separate red and yellow varieties from purple or black varieties by one hundred feet or more. The purple and black bushes can carry viruses that will affect the red and yellow varieties but do no harm to the host bushes.

Mulching is very important. Keep the bushes free of weeds, especially the first year, so the weeds don't rob the bushes of the nutrients and water they need to begin growing. Lay out leaves, wood chips, straw, or hay around the bushes in the summer. Raspberry bushes won't bear a full crop for one to three years after planting. To prune the bushes, pinch off all the blossoms the first year. This helps the plant to fruit the next season. The second year, cut last year's growth back to ground level. Every year after, top the bushes by pruning the tips off the new shoots to prevent sprawling branches and remove all canes older than two years to increase the berry yield next season.

The best way to keep the bushes disease- and pest-free is prevention. Buy only certified, virus-free stock from a reputable nursery. Plant raspberry bushes five hundred to one thousand feet from the nearest wild raspberry bush. Diseases such as Mosaic, Anthracnose, and leaf curl can be spread from the wild bushes. These can't be cured but may be controlled by pruning any damaged canes immediately. Keep the plants clean by removing all the old canes after fruiting, and keep the area free of weeds. As for insects, the only real trouble is with the raspberry cane borer. It lays its eggs at the top of a cane, and the larvae eat through the center until the cane dies. Cutting off all old canes after fruit bearing may prevent this. It will keep the bugs from nesting in the canes over the winter.

Raspberries are best picked and eaten or frozen right away. They are so delicate, they need to be put in shallow containers when harvesting to prevent the fruit from being crushed. Take care when harvesting. Gently pull the fruit from the bush—if it doesn't come off easily, it's not ready to harvest. Most bushes will yield about a pint a piece, so get the whipped cream ready and pick, pick, pick.

 A Scarlet Begonia

TUBEROUS BEGONIAS TAKE center stage in the shade garden, bearing blooms as large as eight inches.

From June through October the flowers, which resemble roses, can have smooth or frilled petals and be single, semidouble, or double. Colors range from shades of yellow and orange to pink and red.

Purchase tubers in midwinter from local garden stores and plant them indoors in pots filled with soilless mix; the tops (which are on the concave side) should barely show above the peat. In the Northeast, the correct time is late February or early March. Move the plants outside to the garden when the weather begins to warm, some time in early June. Begonias prefer shade to partial sunlight and semimoist, rich soil. Keep the plants well watered all summer. The begonias will bloom through fall.

When the frost first causes the foliage to die back, dig up the tubers and store them in plastic bags filled with dry vermiculite, perlite, and peat moss in a cool room until midwinter. Don't wait too long to bring the tubers inside—a complete freeze will kill them. Propagation can be accomplished by dividing the tubers, taking root cuttings, or sowing seeds.

Tuberous begonias are long-lived and, if properly cared for, will produce lovely flowers for years to come.

The Small House at Allington

"Mamma is in the garden," said Bell, with that hypocritical pretence so common with young ladies when young gentlemen call; as though they were aware that mamma was the object specially sought.

"Picking peas, with a sun-bonnet on," said Lily.

"Let us by all means go and help her," said Mr Crosbie; and then they issued out into the garden.

The gardens of the Great House of Allington and those of the Small House open on to each other. A proper boundary of thick laurel hedge, and wide ditch, and of iron spikes guarding the ditch, there is between them; but over the wide ditch there is a footbridge, and at the bridge there is a gate which has no key; and for all purposes of enjoyment the gardens of each house are open to the other. And the gardens of the Small House are very pretty. The Small House itself is so near the road that there is nothing between the dining-room windows and the iron rail but a narrow edge rather than a border, and a little path made with round fixed cobble stones, not above two feet broad, into which no one but the gardener ever makes his way. The distance from the road to the house is not above five or six feet, and the entrance from the gate is shut in by a covered way. But the garden behind the house, on to which the windows from the drawing-room open, is to all the senses as private as though there were no village of Allington, and no road up to the church within a hundred yards of the lawn. The steeple of the church, indeed, can be seen from the lawn, peering, as it were, between the yew-trees which stand in the corner of the churchyard adjoining Mrs Dale's wall. But none of the Dale family have any objection to the sight of that steeple. The glory of the Small House at Allington certainly consists in its lawn, which is as smooth, as level, and as much like velvet as grass has ever yet been made to look. Lily Dale, taking pride in her own lawn, has declared often that it is no good attempting to play croquet up at the Great House. The grass, she says, grows in tufts, and nothing that Hopkins, the gardener, can or will do has any effect upon the tufts. But there are no tufts at the Small House. As the squire himself has never been very enthusiastic about croquet, the croquet implements have been moved permanently down to the Small House, and croquet there has become quite an institution.

Croquet and Other Vigorous Lawn Games

LAWN GAMES HAVE been popular for hundreds of years. All that's needed for an afternoon of fun is some flat lawn space, some simple equipment, and a passing aquaintance with the rules.

Croquet is perhaps the most well-known lawn game. Originating in the British Isles in the nineteenth century, the game was played on well-tended greens with expensive and heavy equipment. Most people have visions of the game being played in the country, with gentlemen in knickers and ladies politely batting the ball around the field. Actually, croquet can be played on any flat backyard surface, whether it is a flourishing, manicured lawn or a scruffy patch of uneven grass.

Today's game uses lightweight, inexpensive, equipment. The basics include the mallet, used to hit the ball; the ball; two stakes, where you begin and end the game; and the wickets, which have curved stakes—usually nine—placed in the ground to create the croquet course. Various layouts can be used for placing the wickets. Typically, a double diamond is set out with a stake at each end. The object of the game is to get the ball through the wickets and to the stake first. This takes physical and strategic skill. Croquet is popular for garden parties, social events, and family get-togethers.

Another popular lawn game is battledore and shuttlecock, more commonly known as badminton. It is thought that this game started in Ancient Greece more than 2,000 years ago. It spread across the Far East to Europe, where medieval peasants played it in the sixteenth century. The upper-class adopted the game as their own in the seventeenth century.

The name *badminton* came from the Duke of Beaufort's residence in England, Badminton House. A new version of battledore and shuttlecock began there in the 1850s and was renamed badminton. This version of the competitive, fast game became popular in the United States in the 1930s. The supplies needed are simple: a birdie (called the shuttlecock in the original game), a rubber and plastic cone that is batted between the players; a couple of rackets (similar to tennis rackets but more lightweight); and a net. The court length should be twice the width. The players—typically two to four—stand on opposite sides of the net and swat the birdie back and forth. The object is to hit the birdie as many times as possible without letting it touch the ground. Participants play the best of three games or up to a preagreed number of points. Men often play to fifteen and women to eleven. It's easy to start a new backyard tradition with this old game.

Lawn bowling, also known as lawn bowls, is a game that can be traced to the Egyptians as early as 5000 B.C. Popular ever since, the bowls has always had devoted admirers. It is said that in 1588, Sir Francis Drake was lawn bowling when informed of the impending arrival of the Spanish Armada. Apparently a great fan, he demanded the game be finished before he left to fight the invaders. While rumor has it that he lost that game, he did win the fight against the Armada. The first game of lawn bowling played in the United States was in the early 1600s. Even George Washington was known to play this game at Mt. Vernon.

Bowls is played with two teams consisting of two to eight players and requires the simple equipment of eight balls (four each of two different colors) and an object ball (smaller than the rest). The object ball is rolled or thrown to one end of the green. The goal of each team is to bowl its balls closest to the object ball. A player can knock his opponents' balls out of the way or even knock the object ball closer to his team's balls. This fun game doesn't require a fancy bowling green; any level patch of grass will do. Lawn bowling can be played at a party or just by two friends who have some time on their hands.

Lawn games take many forms, but they have passed the test of time. Clubs and leagues around the world hold matches and tournaments for the various games. Regardless of your skill level, make your backyard the place to be on the next Fourth of July with more than just a barbecue. Set up the space, pick up that ball, mallet, or racket, and let the games begin.

ANTHONY TROLLOPE

A NICE PIECE of well-maintained lawn can be a point of pride and a delight to the eye. Smooth and velvety, the lawn forms the backdrop to home life: hours spent enjoying picnics, games, cookouts or idling with a good book.

Lawns are created for different purposes. Some are for appearance, some to be used, and others a little of both. For a high-quality lawn in cool climates, use Kentucky bluegrass, perennial ryegrass, and/or red fescue. In warm areas, use cultivars of common Bermuda grass. For a lawn that stands up to kids, games, and entertaining, sow hard-wearing grasses. In cool areas, use perennial ryegrass mixed with red fescue, Kentucky bluegrass, and chewings fescue. In warm areas, sow Bermuda grasses, St. Augustine grass (good for saline conditions), or *Zoysia tenuifolia*, which never needs mowing. All grasses essentially require full sun. While so-called "shade" mixes are available, growing a good lawn in shade is difficult at best. In low light situations, consider an alternate ground cover.

Routine lawn care is very important. Mowing must be done regularly, typically once a week. However, during the growing season, early spring through early summer, it may be necessary to mow even more often. Don't mow in times of drought, wet, or cold. Always wear shoes, gloves, and goggles, and keep your hands away from the blade. When mowing, don't remove more than half of the blade growth at any one time. Lawns can be cut as low as a quarter inch but will then require more frequent mowing. Grass on lawns designed to be used heavily should be kept longer. A low cut is hard on grass; it will cause it to dry out more quickly and will need more watering. Mow in a uniform pattern to save time and create a tidy appearance. When mowing game fields, vary the direction of mowing to keep a grain from developing. Grass clippings can be left on the lawn as fertilizer if you use a mulching mower. Just make sure no large clumps remain.

For the most part, grass is highly drought-resistant, though it will turn brown in hot, dry spells, only to become green again as soon as the weather turns cooler or there is precipitation. If uniform color is desired, constant watering will be necessary; one may want to consider a sprinkler system. In extremely dry climates you may also want to consider reducing the lawn's size to conserve costly water.

Fertilize the lawn three times a year, in early spring, summer, and fall/winter, with supplements of nitrogen, phosphorus, and potassium. The amount of fertilizer required depends on water drainage, rainfall, and your use of grass clippings. Choose a slow-release nitrogen-rich fertilizer that will green up the lawn right away and help it stay green. Be sure to apply the fertilizer evenly with the use of a spreader; heavy clumps of fertilizer can burn the grass.

Other maintenance chores include dethatching, which is the removal of excessive decaying grass, and aerating, a process that prevents the soil from compacting and fosters root growth and development. This latter process is usually done with an aerator, a piece of equipment that can be rented. Or simply tie on golf cleats and go for a walk around the lawn. The spikes on the cleats will puncture the soil in the same manner, though not as deeply.

Weeds can be eliminated through manual or chemical methods. Environmentally friendly weed control, of course, is the preferred method, and many new products are available that virtually eliminate the need for heavy chemical applications. If chemicals are absolutely required, consult with an authority at the local garden center first and keep applications to an absolute minimum. Always read the labels and use the product only as recommended. Wear protective clothing and store chemical products out of reach of children and animals.

Common pests to watch for include grubs, which live in the soil and feed on the grass roots. Moles can also be difficult to deal with. Various methods include trapping them or cutting off their tunnels with sheets of metal. Other diseases and problems that may be encountered include molds, brown patch, red threads, and dollars spot.

On the Eve

Under the lime tree it was cool and peaceful; the bees and flies, when they flew into the circle of its shade, seemed to hum more softly; the clean, slender blades of grass, emerald green with no glint of the sunshine's gold, were still; tall stalks stood motionless, as if bewitched; lifeless, the small clusters of yellow flowers hung from the lower branches of the tree. With every breath a sweet scent seemed to force its way into the lungs, and the lungs drank it up. Far away, beyond the river to the horizon, everything shone and glowed. Sometimes a breeze would stir there and break and intensify the glare; the radiant haze would shimmer above the earth. There was no sound of birds; they do not sing in the heat of the day. But the crickets were chirping everywhere, and it was pleasant to sit at peace in the cool shade and hear that hot sound of life; it inclined to drowsiness and induced dreams.

"Have you noticed," Bersyenev began suddenly, helping out his words with gestures, "what a queer feeling Nature arouses in us? In Nature, everything is so complete, so lucid—I mean so self-satisfying—and we appreciate all that, and admire it; yet at the same time—at least, in me—it always awakens a certain feeling of unrest, anxiety, even of sadness. What does it all mean? Either we are more conscious of our incompleteness, our vagueness when we come face to face with Nature; or else we lack the kind of harmony which satisfies Nature—while the other kind, I mean the kind that we need, Nature hasn't got."

IVAN TURGENEV

The Contemplative Shade Garden 🌿

SEARCHING FOR A corner of solitude—a place for contemplation, to flee with a good book, for quiet conversation, or an overdue respite from a frantic day? Look no farther than your own backyard. You can create a personal oasis beneath the reaching limbs of any established tree by filling its shadow with colorful, soothing, shade-loving plants. In the dappled sunlight, these delightful, easy-care annual and perennial bloomers will mesmerize.

To begin, mark off a wide circle around the tree and build it up by adding topsoil, rotted manure, humus, and compost if available. (Be sure not to raise the soil level around the tree trunk though.) Next, edge the circle with rockery, bricks, or other weather-resistant material. Place the plants in the bed according to height: tall in back, short in front, and all others in between. Mulch and keep the bed well watered until the roots take hold.

Plant a casual mix of flowering leafy plants that will thrive in shade or partial shade. Consider three possibilities: Coleus and caladium will provide bold leaf shapes of exquisite color. A bed of impatiens is simple to care for; just keep it well watered, and you'll have a summer of color. Other low-maintenance bloomers include fluffy-flowered astilbe, easygoing hostas, striking bleeding heart, pale-flowered hellebores, and brilliant begonias. For foliage, ferns bring interest to a shady spot and are virtually care-free. Also try foxgloves, lady's slippers and primula.

To create light-dappled shade best suited for these plantings, trim the crowns of the tree enough so rays of light can find their way through the branches.

A Lime Tree Wherever You Are

LIMES ARE THE most tender of all citrus fruits. They don't hold up well in cold weather and can't be exposed to any frost. Therefore, most of the commercial lime crops are grown in California and Florida, where the trees can be protected. Luckily for gardeners, lime trees can be grown anywhere as an indoor plant, either using a smaller variety or dwarf trees. They can even be transferred outdoors during the warm summer months.

Lime trees come in two principal varieties. The two most common are the Mexican lime (the true lime *Citrus aurantifolia,* also known as the key lime in Florida), and the Bearss lime, which is grown commercially in California. The Bearss lime has fruit slightly larger than the Mexican, about 1½ to 2 inches in diameter. The limes are also seedless. Another fruit, the Rangpur, isn't really a lime at all but a sour Mandarin orange, although it is often sold as a lime tree because its sour fruit so resembles true limes.

A lime tree will only grow as big as its container allows; a sixteen- to twenty-inch container is generally sufficient. Be sure the container has good drainage holes at the bottom. Many mail-order trees will arrive bare-root, so they should be planted immediately. If that isn't possible, keep the roots moist and store in a cool, dark place until planting. Limes will grow in many soil types, but a light commercial potting soil will allow proper drainage for the new plant. Do not add fertilizer to the soil mix when planting. Place the tree in the container and add the potting mix, leaving leaving an inch or two at the top for watering. Water well.

Keeping a lime tree healthy is fairly simple. The main concern is that the plant is receiving sufficient water. Do not let the tree dry out. Water whenever needed, letting the topsoil dry slightly between waterings. (If the tree is outdoors in the summer, this may be daily.) Fertilize with a commercial balanced nitrogen, phosphate, and potash mix several times a year. Humidity is important. If you notice excessive leaf drop, mist the plant with water to elevate the humidity in the area. Lime trees suffer from few pests but may pick up some unwanted visitors from other houseplants, such as scale, mealy bug, and white fly. To deter bugs, wash the leaves frequently with a hose. Try not to use pesticides, as these can render the fruit poisonous and inedible.

A lime tree can be kept indoors all year round, though they prefer to summer outdoors. Limes require full sun. If moving outdoors for the warmer months, place the plant in a shaded area (which may get a few hours of direct sun) for a few weeks before setting out in full sun, to prevent leaf burn. The tree should never be exposed to freezing conditions, so be sure to bring the plant indoors long before any predicted frost.

Limes are actually not at full maturity until they turn yellow. However, the best time to pick limes is when their acidity is at its highest—when they are still green. Squeeze some lime juice over freshly grilled fish for a tangy finish, or just mix up a pitcher of margaritas made with fresh, homegrown limes.

Mail-Order Sources

Four Winds Growers
42786 Palm Avenue
Box 3538
Fremont, CA 94538
www.FourWindsGrowers.com

Lifetime Nursery Products
1866 Sheridan Road
Highland Park, IL 60035

McCann Citrus Nursery
25119 Punkin Center Road
Howey-in-the-Hills, FL 34737
(888)431-LIME

Then we went loafing around town. The stores and houses was most all old, shackly, dried up frame concerns that hadn't ever been painted; they was set up three or four foot above ground on stilts, so as to be out of reach of the water when the river was over-flowed. The houses had little gardens around them, but they didn't seem to raise hardly anything in them but jimpson-weeds, and sunflowers, and ash piles, and old curled-up boots and shoes, and pieces of bottles, and rags, and played-out tinware. The fences was made of different kinds of boards, nailed on at different times; and they leaned every which way, and had gates that didn't generly have but one hinge—a leather one. Some of the fences had been white-washed some time or another, but the duke said it was in Clumbus' time, like enough. There was generly hogs in the garden, and people driving them out.

❧ *The Junk Garden* ❧

THE JUNK GARDEN is designed to suit individual tastes. The old saying, "Beauty is in the eye of the beholder," takes on a new meaning in this tableau.

Creating a junk garden is a process of making the garden a place of personal satisfaction. It's a space that takes full advantage of collections and the art of display. The odd and unusual, as well as the non-descript and seemingly inappropriate, all qualify for presentation.

For best effect, settle on a theme and begin to develop the idea. Flea markets, tag sales, and attics offer treasure troves of possibility. The trick is to think of new and different ways to use ordinary objects. Consider color, shape, size, and the element of surprise. The hunt is part of the fun.

There is no code to follow in the junk garden, so express yourself. A set of colorful, quirky plates can edge a flower bed, and whimsical figures can punctuate garden paths. Mosaic tiles can be combined to create interesting walkways, and old wire gates can support climbing plants. At first thought, an old claw-foot tub may seem out of place, but it can work. Vignettes are always fun to create: garden settings that tell a story or express a thought or theme. And they can be altered from season to season.

The only rule to follow in creating this garden is to make sure your "junk" can stand up to the weather. Rustproofing and waterproofing may become necessary, and plastic coverings may be used to protect cushions and furniture. Aside from that, there are no limits. So indulge yourself in this special place, where you alone will find your pot of gold.

❧ Facing the Sun ❧

SUNFLOWERS WERE CONSIDERED sacred by ancient Egyptians and Greeks because of the unusual way the flowers reacted to the sun. While people find it difficult to look directly into the sun, sunflowers raise their heads and face it, following the sun during the day, seeming to worship its light and warmth. (Plants that turn toward the sun in this manner are called heliotropes.) Sunflowers are perfect for garden backgrounds or screens and will keep the gardener company throughout the summer and fall. They can be grown in virtually any climate.

Members of the daisy family, sunflowers vary in size and color. The common sunflower sports golden yellow petals from a large black eye and grows anywhere from three to twelve feet. The Sunburst and Monarch are good examples of giant types. Teddy Bear, reaching only two feet and offering compact yellow flower heads, makes a good candidate for borders. The tall Dark Red Beauty and Red Sun feature large flowers with deep red petals and brown centers. For white flowers with deep chocolate-colored centers, try Vanilla Ice or Italian White: These grow to four feet tall and are excellent for borders or screens. Regardless which variety you choose, these flowers will attract birds, who love to nibble on their seeds.

Sunflowers are easy-to-grow annuals, as they can survive in just about any soil and will tolerate drought conditions to an uncommon degree. Sunflowers can even pop up unexpectedly under bird feeders from dropped seeds. Sunflower seeds should be planted in the spring after all danger of frost has passed. Plant them one-half inch deep and about two feet apart. Multiple plantings can be done every two weeks throughout the season to ensure blooms through autumn. Plant in full sun and keep well watered for the best and largest flowers. If a bushy plant with more, smaller blooms is desired, pinch the seedlings to encourage branching.

Check sunflowers regularly for pests and disease. Aphids can attack them, sucking the juice from the plants and stunting their growth. If sunflowers are infested, knock off the aphids with a stream of water from the garden hose. This will take care of the immediate problem. Follow up

MARK TWAIN

213

with a natural insecticide if required. Leaf spot can also occur, producing dark stains on the leaves. Removing diseased leaves and stems will generally contain the problem. Otherwise, a general fungicide can be used.

Sunflowers make excellent cut flowers, allowing the gardener to bring a spot of sunshine indoors.

He told Jotham to go out and harness up the greys, and for a moment he and Mattie had the kitchen to themselves. She had plunged the breakfast dishes into a tin dish-pan and was bending above it with her slim arms bared to the elbow, the steam from the hot water beading her forehead and tightening her rough hair into little brown rings like the tendrils on the traveler's joy.

❧ Traveler's Joy ❧

THE ARTFUL BRILLIANCE of traveler's joy—commonly known as clematis—will cause you (and passersby) to stop and look twice. This hardy plant is available from local garden centers or through garden catalogs. Delicate tendrils carry elaborate flowers that will clothe archways, straggle through hedges, and adorn unsightly buildings, fences, and walls. Clematis's lengthy vines produce fabulous flowers up to nine inches across in a fantasy of color beginning in early summer.

A rampant grower, this old garden charmer will thrive when planted in partial shade or sun in rich, well-drained, alkaline soil. Water well before and after planting, and space plants at least five feet apart. An important first measure: Make sure the intended support is strong and firm. Additional preliminary staking may be necessary to train the new plant to grow onto the main support. Next, dig a hole two times the diameter of the plant container. Add organic matter and a slow-release fertilizer to the soil. Place the plant in the hole, making sure the root ball is level with the ground. A handful of lime is generally much appreciated in average or acidic soil. Fill the hole with the soil, then water, and add mulch, which will keep the roots shaded.

Apply fertilizer in the spring during the first two growing seasons. Afterward, a slow-release fertilizer should be applied each year. Keep the plant watered and mulched during dry spells. Deadhead flowers as they fade, and tie new shoots to the support as they grow. When the weather turns cold, wrap clematis with a protective covering.

There are three types of clematis and specific methods for pruning each variety. The first very early-flowering species blooms on last year's wood; they should be pruned after flowering only if the plant has become overgrown. The second, large-flowering mid-season cultivars, bloom on current growth. Cut healthy stems of this variety to just above a strong pair of leaf buds when required. The third, late-flowering species, bloom on the current season's growth and should be pruned in early spring before new shoots appear to remove old, dead growth. For more variety-specific information, it is advisable to check with the local garden center for plant and pruning recommendations.

The House of Mirth

The afternoon was perfect. A deeper stillness possessed the air, and the glitter of the American autumn was tempered by a haze which diffused the brightness without dulling it.

In the woody hollows of the park there was already a faint chill; but as the ground rose the air grew lighter, and ascending the long slopes beyond the high-road, Lily and her companion reached a zone of lingering summer. The path wound across a meadow with scattered trees; then it dipped into a lane plumed with asters and purpling sprays of bramble, whence, through the light quiver of ash-leaves, the country unrolled itself in pastoral distances.

Higher up, the lane showed thickening tufts of fern and of the creeping glossy verdure of shaded slopes; trees began to overhang it, and the shade deepened to the checkered dusk of a beech-grove. The boles of the trees stood well apart, with only a light feathering of undergrowth; the path wound along the edge of the wood, now and then looking out on a sunlit pasture or on an orchard spangled with fruit.

Lily had no real intimacy with nature, but she had a passion for the appropriate and could be keenly sensitive to a scene which was the fitting background of her own sensations. The landscape outspread below her seemed an enlargement of her present mood, and she found something of herself in its calmness, its breadth, its long free reaches. On the nearer slopes the sugar-maples wavered like pyres of light; lower down was a massing of grey orchards, and here and there the lingering green of an oak-grove. Two or three red farm-houses dozed under the apple trees, and the white wooden spire of a village church showed beyond the shoulder of the hill; while far below, in a haze of dust, the high-road ran between the fields.

Art in the Garden

A GARDEN JOURNAL creates a lasting account of daily events in the garden, providing a visual journey through the seasons. Keeping a journal summons memories of gardens past—and inklings of those to come.

Rule number one: Keep it simple and easy. The best time to begin a journal is when garden ideas are germinating. The month of January brings a fresh start, and with it come new plans for the garden. That's the time to put your garden dreams on paper: jot down ideas for interesting species and cultivars you wish to try; invent a new border plan or fling an old one to the ash heap with the stroke of a pencil; build a pool, or sketch out a new deck. Whatever you choose, when spring arrives, the garden plan will be ready. Then, passing garden delights can be documented in words or pictures, with pencil or paintbrush. Feel free to include photos, pressed leaves and flowers or magazine clippings, or even a line drawing of a blooming daffodil or a gentle watercolor of a meadow scene. From spring to summer to fall, as the garden unfolds, page by page the journal will, too.

There are many reasons to keep a garden journal. It's fun to record how a garden grows. Whether studying a single plant or a countryside scene, the journal-keeper will find it a constant source of reference and inspiration. Record keen observations, ideas and recommendations from fellow gardeners. And taking the time to sketch, draw or paint affords a delightful excuse to luxuriate amid the sweet smells and beautiful blossoms.

Of course, there are practical reasons to record a garden's life. Sketching how plants will look together will help prevent poor placement. Recording problems such as pests and poor soil will aid the gardener in refining his or her technique in following seasons. And over time, the journal will make it clear where plants are happiest in the garden.

Faithful cultivation of a garden journal will be its own lasting reward—a personal storehouse of garden pleasures, past and future.

The Lingering Summer Garden

IN MID- TO late summer as the sun climbs higher into the sky, the garden begins its slow coast to a lull. Flowers wane under the weight of the heat, and no matter how brilliant their command performance had been up to this moment, they simply begin to fade away. This is often a turning point for the gardener. After several months of gardening pleasure, the flowering landscape in midsummer becomes dull as the once vibrant and colorful plants wither and droop. Many a gardener has been known to lose interest at this juncture, which is shameful after all the garden has done for him, but it happens nonetheless.

To energize the garden and prevent a midsummer malaise, plan to incorporate a variety of late bloomers in the garden setting. These bright, vivid flowers will invigorate and energize flower beds and borders as other parts of the garden begin their retreat from the stage.

Note the empty or unsatisfying spaces that need to be filled. Note also the height of the current plants at maturity, existing color combinations, and light exposure. Empty spots can quickly be filled with mature plants. However, if seed is to be planted, it needs to be done well ahead of the time you expect your latecomer onstage. And deadheading and other garden-tending gestures are as critical in these later stages of the summer garden as they are in the glorious beginning. These are all important considerations that will keep the garden in constant bloom.

Following are a whole range of mid- to late-summer blooming all-stars, just waiting to be asked to join the show. These stalwarts will carry the essence of summer through the fall, keeping the garden in continual flower.

Aster	Clematis
Blue heliotrope	Coneflower
Bottonia	Coreopsis
Campanula	Feverfew
Chrysanthemum	Gaillardia

Hosta
Hydrangea (peegee, French blue)
Japanese anemones
Lamb's ears
Lavatera
Lobelia
Monarda

Phlox
Roses
Rudbeckia
Salvia
Sedum
Stokesia

Following are suggested groups of flowers to plant together (all bloom until frost):

1. *Midsummer garden:* coreopsis moonbeam, monarda, shasta daisy or aster, cornflower, baby's breath, cosmos, scabiosa, marigold, zinnia or coneflower, coreopsis, dianthus, rudbeckia, scabiosa, sedum autumn joy
2. *Late-summer garden:* torenia, nierembergia, salvia farinacea, nicotiana, snapdragon
3. *Fall garden:* zinnia, cleome, cornflower, cosmos, marigold, nasturium
4. *Everlasting garden:* strawflower, xeranthemum, statice sinuatum, nigella, globe amaranth, starflower

Rebecca of Sunnybrook Farm

Rebecca walked to school after the first morning. She loved this part of the day's programme. When the dew was not too heavy and the weather was fair there was a short cut through the woods. She turned off the main road, crept through uncle Josh Woodman's bars, waved away Mrs. Carter's cows, trod the short grass of the pasture, with its well-worn path running through gardens of buttercups and white-weed, and groves of ivory leaves and sweet fern. She descended a little hill, jumped from stone to stone across a woodland brook, startling the drowsy frogs, who were always winking and blinking in the morning sun. Then came the "woodsy bit," with her feet pressing the slippery carpet of brown pine needles; the "woodsy bit" so full of dewy morning, surprises,—fungous growths of brilliant orange and crimson springing up around the stumps of dead trees, beautiful things born in a single night; and now and then the miracle of a little clump of waxen Indian pipes, seen just quickly enough to be saved from her careless tread. Then she climbed a stile, went through a grassy meadow, slid under another pair of bars, and came out into the road again, having gained nearly half a mile.

Garden of Buttercups

THE WILD-GROWING BUTTERCUP can also serve as a splendid perennial garden plant, lending sunny magnificence to a bed or border. Natural throughout much of North America, the buttercup's small, cup-shaped yellow blooms appear from late spring to late summer, depending on the climate.

Also known as the Tall Buttercup, *Ranunculus acris* can be grown from seed or division. Seeds take a patient gardener: Start plants the previous fall and allow to winter in a cold frame. Buttercups prefer cool temperature and damp soil; they thrive in full sun.

Gardeners willing to wait a few years can cultivate a low-maintenance lawn or meadow of clover and another member of the buttercup family, the bulbous buttercup, *R. bulbosus*. First, however, the existing perennial grasses, along with any other encroachers, must be destroyed. Till the intended area repeatedly until the soil is clear; then sow a mix of buttercup and clover seeds (*Trifolium pratense*), making certain the mix is zone-appropriate. Add in English daisies (*Bellis perennis*) to achieve a grazed meadow effect. This is not an overnight project; it may take up to three years for the seedlings to grow and become established.

Once established, buttercups spread easily in pastures, growing from one to three feet tall. The leaves and stems of most buttercups contain an acrid sap that irritates animals' mouths and deters pests.

Over time, these buttery capped sprigs will establish themselves freely across any grassy area. So next time the dew is heavy and the weather fair, make time for an amble along that well-worn path of glossy buttercups.

The Palette of Wild Mushrooms

UNLIKE IN EUROPE, mushroom hunting is still a virtually unknown pastime in the United States. But mushroom gathering is a great outdoor activity that can involve the whole family. Learning

KATE DOUGLAS WIGGIN

about, collecting, and identifying wild mushrooms is a rewarding experience that is inexpensive and fun.

Mushrooms are actually the fruit of various fungi, which feed on dead and decaying organic matter. Mushrooms contain no chlorophyll, so they don't need light to grow. Mushrooms start as tiny spores that mature into a fibrous root-like mass called the mycelium. What we call the "mushroom" is actually the fruit of the mycelium, much like the apple is the fruit of the apple tree. When mushrooms mature, the gills beneath the cap open to release spores that are carried off by the wind, insects, or animals to start new colonies.

The basic equipment required to begin mushroom hunting and identification is a flat-bottomed basket or box, a roll of waxed paper, a digging tool, and some paper and a pencil to record your findings. The basket can be made of anything, just as long as it has enough room to stand mushrooms upright after picking. The waxed paper is needed to wrap and protect the mushrooms. Do not use plastic wrap, as this can cause moisture buildup that will break down the mushroom before you get a chance to identify it. A tool such as a trowel or a pocketknife is needed to dig up the mushroom. This will help in identifying it later.

The following tips will make identifying mushrooms easier: First, stop at the library and pick up a good book on mushroom identification. This should give detailed pictorial descriptions of mushrooms.

When hunting, dig up the entire mushroom; don't just pluck what's visible from the ground. The bottom portion is an important piece of the puzzle. Many mushrooms look alike at the top, but the base will help determine exactly what kind it is. If possible, collect mushrooms at different stages of development; many books will describe mushrooms at different stages of growth.

Taking notes about the location and describing the mushroom's color, scent, gills, and cap can help, especially if the picker isn't able to identify the mushrooms right away. Finally, after returning home, make a spore print of the mushroom. To do this, cut the cap of the mushroom off the base. Put the cap gill side down on a white piece of paper. Cover it with a bowl and leave it for a few hours. When the mushroom cap is removed from the paper, it will leave behind a distinctive spore print. The spore print is an easy way to start identifying the mushroom, as the color of the spores (invisible singly to the naked eye) is a sure clue to its identity.

Mushrooms come in all colors ranging from creamy white to yellow ochre, rusty brown, and olive brown. Certain species' colors are more affected by moisture and sunlight and are richly pigmented in vivid orange, yellow, scarlet red, and emerald green.

Keep in mind that not all mushrooms are edible. In fact, a small group is poisonous. Be sure never to eat a wild mushroom until it has been accurately identified by an expert.

Mushroom hunting can be a relaxing way to spend time outside. Most mushrooms thrive in the spring and fall, perfect times for a trek into the woods. And many nature centers sponsor mushroom hunting walks. So pack up the kids, the gear, and the books and discover what some people have known for a long time: Wild mushrooms are wonderful hidden pieces of nature just waiting to be found.

KATE DOUGLAS WIGGIN

"Devoted Friend"

"Once upon a time," said the Linnet, "there was an honest little fellow named Hans."

"Was he very distinguished?" asked the Water-rat.

"No," answered the Linnet, "I don't think he was distinguished at all, except for his kind heart, and his funny round good-humoured face. He lived in a tiny cottage all by himself, and every day he worked in his garden. In all the country-side there was no garden so lovely as his. Sweet-william grew there, and Gilly-flowers, and Shepherds'-purses, and Fair-maids of France. There were damask Roses, and yellow Roses, lilac Crocuses, and gold, purple Violets and white. Columbine and Ladysmock, Marjoram and Wild Basil, the Cowslip and the Flower-de-luce, the Daffodil and the Clove-Pink bloomed or blossomed in their proper order as the months went by, one flower taking another flower's place, so that there were always beautiful things to look at, and pleasant odours to smell.

"Little Hans had a great many friends, but the most devoted friend of all was big Hugh the Miller. Indeed, so devoted was the rich Miller to little Hans, that he would never go by his garden without leaning over the wall and plucking a large nosegay, or a handful of sweet herbs, or filling his pockets with plums and cherries if it was the fruit season.

"'Real friends should have everything in common,' the Miller used to say, and little Hans nodded and smiled, and felt very proud of having a friend with such noble ideas."

PLANTING A GARDEN that gracefully rolls out over the season is no easy feat. Some gardeners spend a lifetime, season after season, trying to get the plants and conditions and timing right to create a seemingly effortlessly unfolding garden. And some never get it quite right. But with a firm yet flexible plan in hand, an unfolding display of constant bloom can be designed and implemented by any keenly interested gardener.

To start with, keep it simple and follow the seasons. Nature has always had a good plan, easy to follow and already in place. It can also be adapted to any garden setting. Yellow and white appear in early spring followed by rose in late spring to early summer. Midsummer brings blue and yellow, and then scarlet, gold, and purple color the fall.

If your garden plot is a stage to this unfolding garden, the location of this stage is important. Choose a site that receives at least six hours of sun a day. Lift and turn the soil over, add compost and seasoned manure for nutritional additives. Plan to water well after planting and to mulch to control weeds and conserve moisture. And, as ever, take seriously the planting instructions (regarding zone or required sunlight) that come with your plants or seeds. In other words, make the conditions optimal so you're not hampering your own efforts from the start.

Next, make a plan. Like good soil preparation, time up front planning the garden is a worthy investment that will reap great rewards. Get your plan down on paper if possible, marking plants with X's and O's in various sizes. Think of each of the prospective plants as members of a choir who are carefully situated in the choir loft for a six-month-long concert. They need to work in sync, not against each other, and there needs to be harmony. Consider color preferences, early-, mid- or late-season bloom time, and flower placement—tall in back, short in front, medium in the middle. Attempting for everything to be planted in the right place in relation to the other will make for a good beginning.

Understand that nothing is written in stone; you can always move or remove plants that are just not working the way you had anticipated. In fact, half the fun is in the tinkering, watching the plants from spring to summer to fall, or from year to year, and shuffling them around a bit to greater effect—and even adding new ones. Do give the plants a full cycle or two to show you their stuff—they need the chance to establish themselves and perform before you decide to give them the hook.

Consider the following possibilities and personal favorites of your own. Remember, the strategy is to plant in layers so one plant or group of plants will take center stage as another leaves, creating a quiet ebb and flow through the season.

Here's just one possible cast of characters in this garden drama: tulips and wisteria followed by delphinium, field poppies, early white phlox, and a border of woundwort, and creeping phlox. Next, oriental poppies, lyme grass, gray pink valerian; then hollyhocks, mullein, and fleabane. Finally, Michaelmas daisies for a benediction.

Or try early tulips, daffodils, lavender blue hyacinths followed by Sweet William, Canterbury bells, iris, foxglove, then hollyhocks, goat's rue, phlox, and monkshood.

Or daffodils, aubrietia, tulips, silene acaulis, then columbines, mullein pinks, and true mulleins. Then acoinites and torch lilies.

Or daffodils, tulips, sandwort (*Arenaria montana*), then iris, valerian, and columbine. Next come the tiger lilies, mulleins (*Verbascum phlomoides*), day lilies, veronica, belleflowers, globe thistles.

Or try Canterbury bells, lupines, and iris followed by phlox, silver thistles, daisies, lyme grass, hardy aster, and thistles.

Or pansies, daffodils, grape hyacinths, honesty, and tulips; then iris, daisies, phlox, and roses. Followed by honeysuckle, hollyhocks, veronica, coneflower, and black-eyed Susans, more roses, then chrysanthemums and barberry.

Keep a journal handy and take a few minutes each week to record what's in bloom. Write down the habits, scents, shape, form, and overall appearance of the garden. Jot down dreams or disappointments, plants you've seen elsewhere that you covet for your own garden, or general improvements that might be made. This information will be extremely helpful during the winter months when the *real* garden daydreaming and planning is going on. Your notes and wish lists will help you not repeat mistakes and will provide clues that help you figure out how to fill a time or space or color gap in your unfolding garden.

The unfolding garden is truly the aspirational garden, perhaps a lifelong work-in-progress. As this garden progresses through the seasons and through the years, it will come to naturally unfold in a continuous parade of shape and color, creating interest, harmony, and a mighty pretty picture. So keep your camera ready for the moment you finally get it right.

Shepherd's Purse and Other Quirky Flowers of Yesteryear

NOT EVERYONE CAN live in a quaint, old-fashioned cottage, but anyone can enjoy the beauty, charm, and fragrance of old-fashioned flowers grown in a border, on a patio, or even on a sunny windowsill.

The names of these beauties are as quaint as the time in which they were first cultivated: Sweet William, Cowslip, Shepherd's Purse, Clove Pink. Many of these types of plants are readily available and easy to grow, lending a simple beauty to the garden.

Fig. 1
Sweet William

The hardy biennial Sweet William, or *Dianthus barbatus*, produces colorful, spicy-smelling blooms that look lovely in a border or a cutting bed (its cut flowers are long-lasting) and can easily thrive in a container. The clusters of delicate, saw-toothed blossoms can be grown from a mature plant or from seeds. The flowers are red, pink, or white—often in variations—and bloom in the summer, providing a striking contrast to the plant's thick, stiff, grasslike foliage. Sweet William enjoys full sun. Different varieties grow

Fig. 2
Columbine

from a few inches to a foot-and-a-half tall. As with most flowers, dead-heading prolongs bloom production.

Cultivars of the European Columbine (*Aquilegia vulgaris*) are sure to impress all who see them. Grown in Europe for centuries, countless cultivars are now available. Most have blue, purple, or white flowers (some are doubles) with dainty dangling spurs that bloom from May through July. Hardy from Zones 2 to 3, columbines can be grown from seed, division or purchase of potted specimens.

Shepherd's Purse, *Capsella bursa-pastoris*, is a European native and member of the mustard family that has become naturalized here and now commonly grows in the countryside along roadsides and in lawns throughout the United States. Its interesting name is derived from the shape of the capsule. Small white flowers are produced in clusters that later give way to wedge-shaped capsules reminiscent of the purses carried long ago by shepherds across Europe.

Fig. 3
Shepherds' Purse

Cowslip, *Caltha palustris*, also known as marsh-marigold, is a member of the buttercup family. Fragrant yellow flower stalks arise from the plant in early spring; both the leaves and stalks then die back to the ground by mid-summer, making cowslips a perfect addition to the early spring border. It

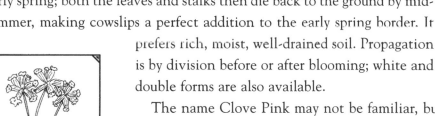

prefers rich, moist, well-drained soil. Propagation is by division before or after blooming; white and double forms are also available.

Fig. 4
Cowslip

The name Clove Pink may not be familiar, but you will certainly recognize the flower as the carnation (*Dianthus caryophyllus*). Technically, the carnation is a perennial, but because it's only hardy to Zone 8, it is often treated as an annual. Though it's unlikely you'll be able to grow the kinds of carnations you see at the florist—those are cultivated in greenhouses—there are a few types referred to as "hardy" or "border," such as Dwarf Fragrance, which can be grown in containers. You'll want to start the seeds indoors for blooms four to six months later. These picky flowers will need full sun, consistent watering and staking. Also, be on the lookout for pests (aphids and spider mites especially) and viral or fungal infections.

This season, include a few of these beauties among your modern cultivars. Their quaintness will hearken to simpler times, lending an old-fashioned elegance to the garden.

Oscar Wilde

The Picture of Dorian Gray

The studio was filled with the rich odour of roses, and when the light summer wind stirred amidst the trees of the garden there came through the open door the heavy scent of the lilac, or the more delicate perfume of the pink-flowering thorn.

From the corner of the divan of Persian saddle-bags on which he was lying, smoking, as was his custom, innumerable cigarettes, Lord Henry Wotton could just catch the gleam of the honey-sweet and honey-coloured blossoms of a laburnum, whose tremulous branches seemed hardly able to bear the burden of a beauty so flamelike as theirs; and now and then the fantastic shadows of birds in flight flitted across the long tussore-silk curtains that were stretched in front of the huge window, producing a kind of momentary Japanese effect, and making him think of those pallid jade-faced painters of Tokio who, through the medium of an art that is necessarily immobile, seek to convey the sense of swiftness and motion. The sullen murmur of the bees shouldering their way through the long unmown grass, or circling with monotonous insistence round the dusty gilt horns of the straggling woodbine, seemed to make the stillness more oppressive. The dim roar of London was like the bourdon note of a distant organ.

Languorous Lilac

LILAC AND LABURNUM, two old-fashioned ornamental bloomers, provide a colorful welcome to spring with their feathery blossoms. These hardy and tenacious shrubs tolerate cold conditions but don't object to mild winters and hot summers. Laburnum is a good choice for small gardens since it dutifully contains its hardy exuberance.

Lilacs should be planted in a prominent position where their lavish display can be admired. They look stunning as hedges. Laburnum, which tolerates exposed and windy sites, is just as striking, bending toward the ground with the weight of its honey-colored blossoms, which resemble wisteria. Lilacs can be grown in Zones 3 to 8, and laburnum makes its home in Zones 5 to 9.

Lilacs and laburnum should be planted in a hole twice as wide as the root ball. This will allow the roots to spread out and gather nourishment. Work several shovelsful of well-rotted organic matter into the soil you've removed; for the lilac, also add a handful or two of lime. Place the plant in the hole at the same level it was in the container and refill. Water regularly until the roots are established. Fertilize once a year with 10-10-10 or the equivalent. A top layer of shredded mulch will keep the roots moist and prevent unwelcome weeds that rob the plant of its nourishment. For best bloom, remove the spent flower heads to conserve vital nutrients for next year's blossoms. Prune as required to remove old, diseased, or weak stems.

Lilacs are easy to cut and look spectacular when used in arrangements. (Just remember that the branches you cut this year won't flower the next, so be sure to spread your cutting over a wide area.) Once brought inside, their delicious fragrance will perfume the air. When arranging lilacs, pick blossoms early in the morning or late in the evening. Fill a bucket with cold water and plunge the cut flowers neck-deep immediately to prevent wilting. Keep the flowers in water until you are ready to use them. Before arranging the blossoms, strip the leaves below the water line. Then, either crush the stem or slit it with a sharp pair of pruning shears and place the stems in a container. While slightly less fragrant, the white varieties seem to last the best indoors.

Look Homeward, Angel: A Story of the Buried Life

Oliver married Eliza in May. After their wedding trip to Philadelphia, they returned to the house he had built for her on Woodson Street. With his great hands he had laid the foundations, burrowed out deep musty cellars in the earth, and sheeted the tall sides over with smooth trowellings of warm brown plaster. He had very little money, but his strange house grew to the rich modelling of his fantasy: when he had finished he had something which leaned to the slope of his narrow uphill yard, something with a high embracing porch in front, and warm rooms where one stepped up and down to the tackings of his whim. He built his house close to the quiet hilly street; he bedded the loamy soil with flowers; he laid the short walk to the high veranda steps with great square sheets of colored marble; he put a fence of spiked iron between his house and the world.

Then, in the cool long glade of yard that stretched four hundred feet behind the house he planted trees and grape vines. And whatever he touched in that rich fortress of his soul sprang into golden life: as the years passed, the fruit trees—the peach, the plum, the cherry, the apple—grew great and bent beneath their clusters. His grape vines thickened into brawny ropes of brown and coiled down the high wire fences of his lot, and hung in a dense fabric, upon his trellises, roping his domain twice around. They climbed the porch end of the house and framed the upper windows in thick bowers. And the flowers grew in rioting glory in his yard—the velvet-leaved nasturtium, slashed with a hundred tawny dyes, the rose, the snowball, the redcupped tulip, and the lily. The honey-suckle drooped its heavy mass upon the fence; wherever his great hands touched the earth it grew fruitful for him.

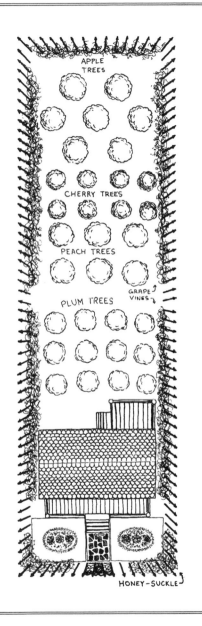

❧ Gant's Yard ❧

OLIVER GANT WAS a true American product of his late Victorian times. This is to say he was greatly concerned with presenting a home and property that projected his status in the community—or at least the status to which he aspired: businessman, family man, role model. In the end, Gant wasn't much of any of these, but he built the house and yard of a man who was.

The Victorian sensibility regarding neighborhood and property called for an attention to the collective aesthetic. One no longer considered his property myopically or selfishly, but instead considered it with an eye toward some uniformity in relation to the other homes on the street. In fact, this period introduced the idea of neighborhood and the way in which each home and property worked together as a part of the big picture. Each house and yard was not meant to be the same as the other, but each was certainly expected to make a not dissimilar and eye-pleasing contribution. One could say, even, that the period introduced the middle-class "keeping up with the Joneses" approach to yard and garden.

Gant's yard toed the late Victorian line in all the most important ways. In the front of the house were ornate flower beds, thick with nasturtium, roses, snowball, tulips and lilies. There was also an elaborate walkway and a honeysuckle-drenched "fence of spiked iron between him and the world."

His amazing gift in the garden made itself most apparent in the backyard. He had exceedingly good soil and an extremely green thumb—on a modest plot of land, he planted fruit trees and grapevines with joyous abandon, and they thrived beyond measure. Over time, the vines burst their trellised bounds, climbed toward the porch, and created a glorious frame for the house. And his backyard orchard of apple, peach, cherry, and plum trees was surely the envy of his neighbors.

Despite his hearty attempts to rise to the occasion, poor Gant always remained wedged between his working-class roots and his middle-class aspirations. To wit, unlike most of his somewhat better-heeled neighbors, he built his home and planted his yard with his own big hands. Still, through his lifetime of (mostly self-inflicted) turmoil, he found great solace in the monument of his mighty orchard and loamy flower beds.

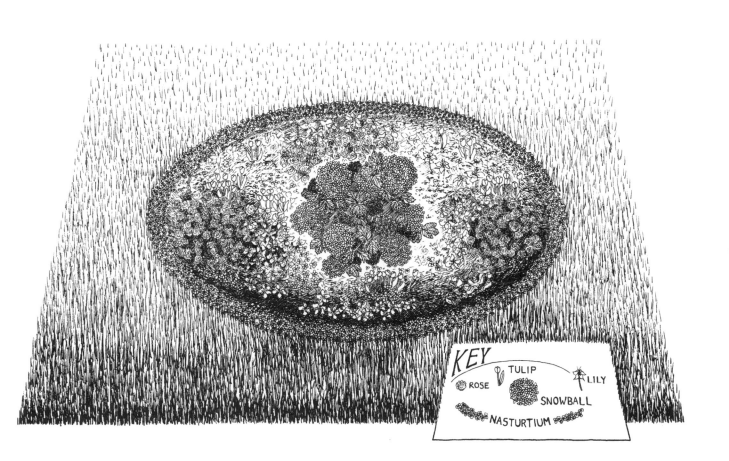

KEY

ROSE · TULIP · LILY
SNOWBALL
NASTURTIUM

The plum-tree, black and brittle, rocks stiffly in winter wind. Her million little twigs are frozen in spears of ice. But in the Spring, lithe and heavy, she will bend under her great load of fruit and blossoms. She will grow young again. Red plums will ripen, will be shaken desperately upon the tiny stems. They will fall bursted on the loamy warm wet earth; when the wind blows in the orchard the air will be filled with dropping plums; the night will be filled with the sound of their dropping, and a great tree of birds will sing, burgeoning, blossoming richly, filling the air also with warm-throated plum-dropping bird-notes.

PLUM TREES CAN be grown in almost any temperate climate. It's important, though, to pay attention to culture and zone guidelines when ordering and buying, as certain varieties do far better in some areas than others.

Plum tree varieties are generally divided into three categories. The European, including Mt. Royal, Stanley Prune and Green Gage, grow best from Zones 5 to 9. Japanese plum varieties, such as Abundance, Burbank, Formosa and Red Heart need warmer climates. These should be grown from Zones 6 to 9. The American hybrids are the hardiest of the three. Ember, Pipestone, and Superior survive in Zones 4 through 8. Rule of thumb: European and American hybrid varieties are about as hardy as apples, while Japanese varieties more resemble peaches. Most plum trees will naturally grow up to twenty feet tall, though smaller dwarf versions of common varieties are available. Be sure to buy at least two varieties in each category to ensure good cross-pollination.

Plan to plant plum trees in early spring, just as soon as the soil can be easily worked. In warmer climates, fall is also a good time to plant. Allow twenty feet between trees, less for dwarf or bushy varieties. Select a site with great sun and good drainage. Dig a hole a foot wider than the root spread and plant with the roots fanned out. Be sure the tree sits at the same level it did at the nursery. Fill the hole halfway with soil, water well and then finish filling the hole and water again. Mulch generously.

Fertilize annually with 10-10-10 or an organic equivalent. Be sure plenty of water is available throughout the spring and summer, especially during the flowering and fruit-bearing time. Plum trees won't fruit until the third or fourth year. Be patient, though, because once it happens, those juicy plums will continue coming for fifteen years or more. Very early spring, before the sap rises, is the best time to prune. The general goal in pruning is to let light into the tree, for it is critical for the growth of the fruit and helps prevent the tree from becoming overloaded with plums.

Beware of plum curculio. These insects lay their eggs within the fruit. They then hatch and eat the plum from the inside out. If the tree is infested, the fruit will begin to fall off prematurely and the remaining fruit will have black rot marks on the skin. One reported method to rid the tree of beetles is to shake them off the tree onto a tarp below. Continue shaking every other day until there are no more beetles falling off and the fruit is clean. Spraying the tree with low-toxicity pesticide will also get rid of the beetles. Beware also of black knot, a fungus evident by dark, swelling lumps on the branches. Aggressively cut back the affected branches and keep a vigilant eye for recurrence or spread to other trees.

Plums are ready to harvest when a gentle twist is all it takes to remove them from the tree. Then it's time to sit back and enjoy the sweet taste of plum success.

Sources

Miller Nurseries
West Lake Road
Canandaigua, NY 14424
(800) 836-9630

Henry Leuthardt Nurseries, Inc.
Montauk Highway, Box 666
East Moriches, NY 11940

New York State Fruit Testing Cooperative Association
Geneva, NY 14456
(315) 787-2205

Nana

Madame did not hear what she said. Leaning over the balustrade, she was gazing at the grounds below her. They consisted of seven or eight acres of land, enclosed within a wall. Then the sight of the kitchen garden seized her attention. She darted back into the house and pushed past the maid on the stairs, stammering:

"It's full of cabbages!... You've never seen such big cabbages!... And lettuces, and sorrel, and onions, and everything! Come quick!"

The rain was falling more heavily now. She opened her white silk parasol, and ran down the garden walks.

"Madame will catch cold," shouted Zoé, who had stayed safely under the glass porch over the steps.

But Madame wanted to see, and at each new discovery there was an exclamation.

"Zoé, there's spinach! Do come and see... Oh! Artichokes! They are funny. So artichokes have flowers, do they?... Now, what can that be? I've never seen that before.... Do come, Zoé, perhaps you know."

The maid did not budge. Madame must be raving mad. For now the rain was coming down in torrents, and the little white silk parasol was already completely black; it didn't shelter Madame either, and her skirts were wringing wet. Not that that seemed to bother her. In the pouring rain she toured the kitchen garden and the orchard, stopping in front of every tree, and bending over every bed of vegetables. Then she ran and looked down the well, lifted up a frame to see what was underneath it, and became engrossed in the contemplation of a huge pumpkin. She felt an urge to go along every path in the garden, and to take immediate possession of all things she had dreamt of in the old days, when she had been a poor working-girl in Paris. The rain was getting heavier, but she did not feel it, her only complaint being that the daylight was fading. She could not see clearly any longer, and had to touch things with her fingers to find out what they were. All of a sudden, in the twilight, she made out a bed of strawberries, and all the longings of her childhood burst forth.

"Strawberries! Strawberries! There are some here: I can feel them!... A plate, Zoé. Come and pick strawberries."

And Nana squatted in the mud, dropping her parasol and exposing herself to the full force of the downpour. Her hands dripping with water, she began picking strawberries among the leaves.

❧ The Kitchen Garden ❧

THE PLEASURE OF dressing the dinner table with a fresh assortment of fruits, herbs, and vegetables harvested from your own property is a terrific incentive to plant a kitchen garden. Savory garden delicacies whet the appetite, and the just-picked freshness of your own crops greatly enhances their nutritional value, since valuable vitamins haven't had time to escape. Whether you just plan to enjoy the produce seasonally or to plant enough for canning, freezing, or drying, growing a kitchen garden is a rewarding endeavor.

To begin, select a garden site. The ideal site is close to the kitchen and a water supply—important considerations for a practical garden—and in full sun. The location also needs to be well-drained, so avoid low spots where water will collect.

Next, make a plan. Remember, in the kitchen garden, allow form to follow function. A typical kitchen garden plan is an arrangement of rectangular beds crossed by pathways. Vegetables can be planted in short rows or beds around the paths. Narrow plantings intersected by paths are easy to work from; each bed can be planted, weeded, and harvested from all sides, and there's no need to muck about in the soil. The paths need to be large enough to accommodate a wheelbarrow and can be carpeted with grass, covered by gravel, or laid with brick or stone.

Your plantings should be positioned with height in mind so that they won't shade each other. Plant the tall crops, such as corn or staked tomatoes, on the north side of the garden or toward the rear. Place low-growing vegetables in front, and consider shapes, textures, and colors when planning the plot. Cutting flowers are often intermingled or planted along the borders to add a splash of color.

Plant only what you'll use. It only makes sense to plant fruits, herbs, and vegetables that the family will enjoy. This will keep your interest level high and eliminate wasted time and produce. Consult with garden catalogs and local garden centers to select seed or plant varieties. Look for types that are disease-resistant, productive, and flavorful. Try to plant so the garden will yield a steady supply of produce once production begins. This can be accomplished by planting early and

ÉMILE ZOLA

late varieties together or sowing small batches at one- to two-week intervals.

To prepare the soil, lift all sod with a flat-edged shovel or turn it under with a garden tiller. Turn the soil over and add soil amendments such as compost, manure, or other organic material and mix in thoroughly. It is advisable to conduct a soil test to determine what other elements or trace minerals are needed. These test kits are sold at local garden centers and are available through horticulture extension agents. If your soil is too hard or rocky, a good option is to build raised beds. These beds are then filled with topsoil and soil amendments and are tidy, attractive, and easy to maintain.

Weeding and watering should be done as needed, though twenty minutes a day should suffice. A well-tended garden will be productive and attractive all season if it is properly maintained. Some gardeners prefer to invest in an irrigation system, whether it be a simple soaker hose, an underground or above-ground sprinkler, or a trickle drip-feed.

Basic tools to have on hand include a spading fork, rake, hoe, watering can, garden spade or round pointed shovel, stakes, string, and gloves. Other handy items are a wheelbarrow, hose, soaker hose, and sprinkler. Buy the best equipment you can afford, and keep tools clean and oiled. Quality tools will last longer and be much easier to use.

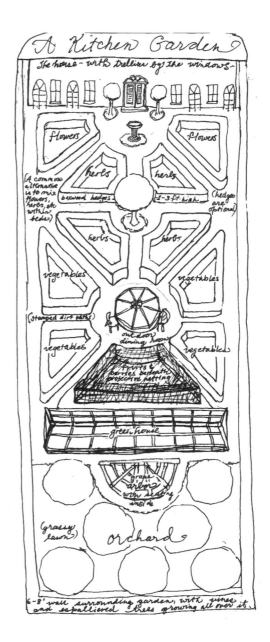

Artichokes!

NATIVE TO THE Mediterranean, artichokes (*cynara scolymus*) are grown commercially on the California coast. The foggy, moist summers and mild winters there create a perfect climate for this edible crop. You don't have to be an expert farmer to cultivate this delicacy. Home gardeners can grow artichoke plants in most climate zones in the United States. They can survive as far north as New York, with some care and protection.

Artichokes are thistlelike plants that grow four to six feet high and three to four feet around. It isn't a plant for the small garden, but it adds interest placed in unexpected areas around the yard, such as against fences and along borders and walkways. The best way to grow artichokes is to acquire a sucker from an established plant. These can be purchased at a nursery or garden center or taken from another artichoke plant in the spring. Starting seeds taken from existing plants isn't recommended: seeds vary greatly and may result in poor-quality plants.

While technically hardy to Zone 5, artichokes require special attention in colder areas, and may be grown there as an annual. Imperial Star and Grande Beurre have been especially bred for colder one-season growing zones, maturing in five months, compared to up to seven months for perennial types.

Artichokes should be planted in the spring, after all danger of frost is past. Diseases and pests rarely affect artichokes—though you should still watch out for aphids. Soil is the key. It should be very fertile with good drainage as the roots are prone to rotting. Work rotted manure and compost deeply before planting.

Annual varieties will produce buds the first year. Perennials won't yield the edible buds until the second year. Established plants will produce about ten buds per season. During the first season, the small buds on the perennial types should be nipped off to encourage growth for the next spring. Mulch heavily around artichoke plants to keep out weeds, and keep them moist during dry spells. Fertilize with a nitrogen-rich mixture just as the buds start to form and then again right after harvest. After harvesting, the yellowed stalks should be cut back to within an inch or two of the ground. In areas with hard ground freeze, the perennial artichoke should be sheltered for

ÉMILE ZOLA

the winter. Cover the stalks with wood ashes and place a protective covering of wood or plastic over them.

Artichokes should be harvested before the bracts, or leafy scales, have begun to pull away from the bud. When these start to open, the bud becomes tough and woody. If the bud has flowered, it's too late to harvest at all—simply enjoy the purplish thistle heads. Cut the central bud first, about three to four inches from the base. Then proceed to take off the buds appearing from the side branches. Later in the season, brown spots may occur on the leaves due to light frost damage, but this will not affect the taste of the artichoke.

While artichokes are not as common in gardens as tomatoes, in the right climate they can be grown and managed just as easily. One taste of the tender artichoke should convince any wary gardener to make a space for this unusual vegetable.

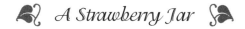 *A Strawberry Jar*

A STRAWBERRY JAR bursting with plump, delicious berries makes a charming addition to any patio, doorway entrance, or garden nook. It can also be used for ornamentation, as a focal point in the garden, or along a pathway, providing added interest. Planting a strawberry jar is easy, fun, and ensures these tasty fruits will be readily available.

To start, collect the following items:

An eighteen- or twenty-inch strawberry jar, available at garden centers or hardware stores
Small fruiting strawberry plants to fill it: one per hole as well as four or five for the top of the pot
Potting soil
A sixteen- or eighteen-inch-long piece of two-inch piping such as PVC, available at building supply stores (the pipe length should be two inches shorter than the height of the post)
A two-inch plastic cap
Small pieces of gravel
Aluminum foil
A rubber band

Since a strawberry jar is deep, it is necessary to create a plumbing system that irrigates all the strawberry plants. To make the irrigation system, drill four holes approximately one-eighth inch in size around the sides of the piping. Begin one inch from the top and repeat every two inches, ending one inch from the bottom of the piping. Cover one end of the piping with the two-inch plastic cap, and fill the pipe with the gravel.

Next, cover the drainage hole in the bottom of the strawberry jar with small pieces of broken clay pots, known as potsherds. There must be enough pieces to prevent the soil from washing away while still allowing the water to drain.

Cover the top of the piping with aluminum foil and fasten with a rubber band. Place the bottom end of the plastic cap on the

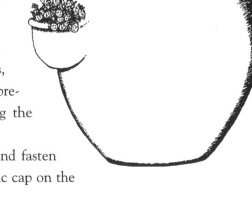

potsherds, making certain the piping stands straight so the water will drain evenly and that the top reaches to just below level of the pot. Fill the pot with enough soil to reach the first level of openings. Set one plant into each first-level opening and add more potting soil, making sure to cover the roots of the plants. Continue to add more soil up to the next level of openings. Set one plant into each first-level opening and add more potting soil, making sure to cover the roots of the plants. Continue to add more soil up to the next level of openings; water the soil. As the potting soil settles, add more. Plant the next level of plants and continue until the entire pot is planted, including the top opening.

Remove the rubber band and aluminum foil and fill the pipe to overflowing with water. The pipe will drain as the water filters to the plants. The strawberry plants can be fertilized in the same manner—pour liquid fertilizer directly into the pipe and let it drain.

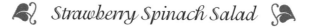

Strawberry Spinach Salad

THERE IS NOTHING that beats garden-fresh strawberries. Watch them ripen and pick them at the peak of perfection. For those who don't grow their own, there are still plenty of fresh berries to be found. Many gardeners set up roadside stands and sell their strawberries, and many areas host pick-them-yourself berry patches. Grocery stores stock fresh strawberries in the summer, and they are usually of good quality. Choose deep red berries that are full and well-shaped. Don't worry if there is still a little white at the top—that's fine; the darker bottom part of the berry can still be sliced and used. Strawberries can be stored in the refrigerator or frozen, but they are best used as soon as possible. Pick them while still warm from the sun and nibble on a few while slicing the others for this salad.

12 oz. spinach, washed, dried, and torn into bite-sized pieces
1 quart fresh strawberries, sliced
2 tablespoons toasted sesame seeds

Dressing:

- ½ cup olive oil
- ¼ cup packed brown sugar
- ¼ cup white sugar
- 1½ tablespoons grated onion
- 1¼ teaspoons paprika
- ½ teaspoon Worcestershire sauce
- ¼ cup red wine vinegar
- 1 tablespoon balsamic vinegar

Mix all dressing ingredients together in a sealed container and shake well. Arrange spinach and strawberries on four plates and top with dressing. Sprinkle toasted sesame seeds over each salad.

YIELD: 4 servings

ÉMILE ZOLA

Aiken, "The Dark City," *The Collected Short Stories of Conrad Aiken*: Out of print.

Alcott, *Little Women*: Penguin USA, 1989.

Anderson, *Winesburg, Ohio*: Penguin Twentieth Century Classics, 1992.

Balzac, *The Country Doctor*: Dutton, 1961, out of print.

Baum, *The Wonderful World of Oz: The Wizard of Oz, The Emerald City of Oz, Glinda of Oz*: Penguin Twentieth Century Classics, 1998.

Brontë, *Jane Eyre*: Penguin Classics, 1996.

Carroll, *Through the Looking-Glass: Alice's Adventures in Wonderland and Through the Looking-Glass: And What Alice Found There*: Penguin USA, 1998.

Cather, *Death Comes for the Archbishop*: Vintage Classics, 1990.

Cather, *My Ántonia*: Penguin USA: Great Books of the Twentieth Century, 1999.

Colette, *Places*: Bobbs Merrill Co., 1971, out of print.

Chestnutt, *The House Behind the Cedars*: Penguin USA, Twentieth Century Classics, 1993.

Dickens, *The Pickwick Papers*: Oxford World Classics, Oxford University Press, 1998.

du Maurier, *Rebecca*: Avon, 1997.

Eliot, *The Mill on the Floss*: Penguin USA, 1987.

Falkner, *Moonfleet*: Ace, 1982, out of print.

Fitzgerald, *Tender Is the Night*: Scribner, 1995.

Forster, *Howards End*: Vintage Books, 1989.

Forster, *Where Angels Fear to Tread*: Vintage Books, 1992.

Hardy, *The Return of the Native*: Penguin Classics: Viking Press, 1978.

Hawthorne, *Blithedale Romance*: The Penguin American Library, 1983.

Hawthorne, "Rappaccini's Daughter," *Selected Tales and Sketches*: Penguin Classics, 1987.

Holmes, *Elsie Venner: A Romance of Destiny*: Ayer Co. Publishing, 1976.

Hugo, *Les Misérables*: Penguin Classics, 1982.

Lawrence, *Sons and Lovers*: Penguin Twentieth Century Classics, 1995.

Mansfield, "Bliss," *Bliss and Other Stories*: Wordworth Collection: Wordworth Editions, Ltd., 1999.

Orczy, *The Scarlet Pimpernel*: Bantam Classics and Loveswept, 1992.

Proust, *Remembrance of Things Past (vol. 1) Swann's Way*: Penguin USA, 1998.

Sandburg, "How to Tell Corn Fairies If You See 'Em," *Rootabaga Stories*: Harcourt Brace, 1990.

Stowe, *Uncle Tom's Cabin*: Penguin USA: The Penguin American Library, 1986.

Trollope, *The Small House at Allington*: Penguin USA, 1993.

Turgenev, *On the Eve*: Viking Press, 1950.

Twain, *The Adventures of Huckleberry Finn*: Bantam Classics, 1981.

Wharton, *Ethan Frome*: Penguin USA: Twentieth Century Classics, 1994.

Wharton, *The House of Mirth*: Penguin USA: Twentieth Century Classics, 1993.

Wiggin, *Rebecca of Sunnybrook Farm*: Puffin Classics, 1995.

Wilde, "Devoted Friend," *Complete Short Fiction*: Penguin USA, 1995.

Wilde, *The Picture of Dorian Gray*: Penguin USA, Penguin Classics, 1986.

Wolfe, *Look Homeward Angel: A Story of the Buried Life*: Scribner, 1995.

Zola, *Nana*: Viking Press, 1985.

❧ LIST OF ILLUSTRATIONS ❧

❧ RESOURCES ❧

Aiken, "The Dark City"
ON MY KNEES BEFORE MY BEANS
    Johnny's Selected Seeds
    Foss Hill Rd.
    Albion, ME 04910
    (207) 437-9294
    www.johnnnyseeds.com

    Vermont Bean Seed Co.
    Garden Lane
    Fair Haven, VT 05743
    (802) 273-3400

RAMPANT STRAWBERRIES
    Allen Plant Company
    PO Box 310
    Fruitland, MD 21826-0310
    (410) 742-7123

    Nourse Farms, Inc.
    41 River Rd.
    Deerfield, MA 01373
    (413) 665-2658
    www.noursefarms.com

Alcott, *Little Women*
FRIENDLY LITTLE NEIGHBORS
    Edmund's Roses
    6235 SW Kahle Rd.
    Wilsonville, OR 97070
    (503) 682-1476
    www.edmundsroses.com

ROSES OF YESTERDAY & TODAY
    803 Brown's Valley Rd.
    Watsonville, CA 95076-0398
    (408) 724-3537

    Rose Petals (or Beyond Potpourri)
    Crabtree & Evelyn
    (800) 272-2873
    www.crabtree-evelyn.com

Anderson, *Winesburg, Ohio*
BEE GARDENS
    For more information: www.wildwords.com

Balzac, *The Country Doctor*
THE ALLEY OF HORNBEAM
    Angelgrove Tree Seed Company
    PO Box 74, Riverhead
    Harbor Brace, NF (Canada) A0A3PO
    (709) 596-2224
    www.nf.sympatico.ca/angelgrove/angelsd.htm

    Elk Mountain Nursery
    142 Webb Cove Rd.
    Asheville, NC 28804
    (828) 251-9622
    www.elk-mountain.com

THE ESPALIER
    Arbor & Espalier
    201 Buena Vista Avenue East
    San Francisco, CA 94117
    (415) 626-8880

Henry Leuthardt Nurseries, Inc.
PO Box 666
Montauk Highway
East Moriches, NY 11940
(516) 878-1387

Baum, *The Wonderful Wizard of Oz*
THE DEADLY POPPY FIELD
  Andre Viette Farm & Nursery
  Route 1 Box 16
  Star Route 608
  Fishersville, VA 22939
  (703) 942-2118

  Garden Place
  PO Box 388
  Mentor, OH 44061-0388
  (216) 255-3705

Bronte, *Jane Eyre*
THE GOOSEBURY BUSH
  Bear Creek Nursery
  PO Box 411
  Northport, WA 99157
  (509) 732-6219
  www.bearcreeknursery.com

  Nourse Farms
  41 River Rd.
  Deerfield, MA 01373
  (413) 665-2658
  www.noursefarms.com

IVY RECESSES
  American Ivy Society
  PO Box 2123
  Naples, FL 33939-2123
  (813) 261-0388

Ivies of the World
PO Box 408
Weirsdale, FL 32195-0408
(904) 821-2201

Carroll, *Through the Looking-Glass*
THE GARDEN OF LIVE FLOWERS and
THE SHRILL LITTLE DAISIES
  The Cook's Garden
  PO Box 535
  Londonderry, VT 05148
  (802) 824-3400

  W. Atlee Burpee Company
  300 Park Ave.
  Westminster, PA 18974
  (800) 888-1447
  http://garden.burpee.com

PASSIONATE TIGER LILIES
  Dutch Gardens
  PO Box 200
  Adelphia, NJ 07710-0200
  (800) 818-3861
  www.dutchgardens.com

  Saxton Gardens
  1 First St.
  Saratoga Springs, NY 12866
  (518) 584-1697

Cather, *Death Comes for the Archbishop*
A BLANKET OF PURPLE VERBENA
  Avant Gardens
  710 High Hill Rd.
  Dartmouth, MA 02747
  (508) 998-8819
  www.avantgardensne.com

W. Atlee Burpee Company
300 Park Ave.
Westminster, PA 18974
(800) 888-1447
http://garden.burpee.com

THE GARDEN PALETTE
Keen, Mary. *Gardening with Color*. New York: Random House, 1991.
Hobhouse, Penelope. *Color in Your Garden*. Boston: Little, Brown, 1985.

PLACEMENT OF FRUIT TREES
Otto, Stella. *The Backyard Orchardist: A Complete Guide to Growing Fruit Trees in the Home Garden*, 1993.

Hill, Lewis. *Fruits & Berries for the Home Garden*. Pownal: Storey Communications, 1992.

Cather, *My Ántonia*
SOMETHING UNDER THE SUN
Glecker Seedmen
Metmaora, OH 43540
(419) 923-5463

Garden.com, Inc.
3301 Steck Ave.
Austin, TX 78757
(800) 466-8142
www.garden.com

THE GARDEN OF AUTUMN GLORY
Mums by Paschke
12286 East Main Rd.
North East, PA 16428
(814) 725-9860

Avant Gardens
711 High Hill Rd.
Dartmouth, MA 02747
(508) 998-8819
www.avantgardensne.com

ORNAMENTAL GRASSES
The Bath Nursery
2432 Cleveland Massillion Rd.
Akron, OH 44333
(330) 659-2080
www.mytownohio.com/tbn

Virtual Seeds Co.
PO Box 684
Selma, OR 97538
www.virtualseeds.com

THE ORCHARD
Plumtree Nursery
387 Springtown Rd.
New Paltz, NY 12561
(914) 255-0417

Tripple Brook Farm
37 Middle Rd.
Southampton, MA 01073
(413) 527-4626

TRAINING A GRAPEVINE
Bay Laurel Nursery
2500 El Camino Real
Atascadero, CA 93422
(805) 466-3406
www.baylaurelnursery.com

Arkansas Berry & Plant Farm
22339 North Hwy. 71
Winslow, AR 72959
(501) 634-7020
www.alcasoft.com/arkansas/

THE CURRANT BUSH
Nourse Farms
41 River Rd.
Deerfield, MA
(413) 665-2658
www.noursefarms.com

One Green World
28696 Cramer Rd.
Molalla, OR 97038-8576
(503) 651-3005
www.onegreenworld.com

Chestnutt, *The House Behind the Cedars*
LOOKING THROUGH CEDARS
Coldstream Farm
2030 West Freesoil Rd.
Freesoil, MI 49411
(616) 464-5809

Elk Mountain Nursery
142 Webb Cove Rd.
Asheville, NC 28804
(828) 251-9622
www.elk-mountain.com

THE LIVING FENCE
Conley's Garden Center
145 Townsend Ave.
Boothbay Harbor, ME 04538
(800) 334-1812

Double D Nursery
2215 Dogwood Lane
Arnoldsville, GA 30619
(800) 438-7685

Colette, *Places*
THE HERB GARDEN THAT BEGS TO BE TOUCHED
Companion Plants
7247 North Coolville Ridge Rd.
Athens, OH 45701
(614) 592-4643
www.frognet.net/companionsplants

Johnny's Selected Seeds
Foss Hill Rd.
Albion, ME 04910-9371
(207) 437-9294
www.johnnyseeds.com

HEIRLOOM TOMATOES
Heirloom Seeds
PO Box 245
West Elizabeth, PA
(412) 384-0852
www.heirloomseeds.com

Totally Tomatoes
PO Box 1626
Augusta, GA 30903
(803) 663-0016

Dickens, *The Pickwick Papers*
THE HUNDRED PERFUMES
Meadowbrook Herb Garden
93 Kingstown Rd.
Wyoming, RI 02898
(401) 539-7603

Select Seeds Antique Flowers
180 Stickney Hill Rd.
Union, CT 06076-4617
(860) 684-9310
www.selectseeds.com

THE BIRD GARDEN
www.wildwords.com

National Wildlife Federation
8925 Leesburg Pike
Vienna, VA 22814-0001
(703) 790-4000
www.nwf.org

du Maurier, *Rebecca*
AN ARMY OF DAFFODILS
Cascade Valley Farms
PO Box 387
Parkdale, OR 97041
(541) 352-7098
www.cascadevalley farms.com

WildBloomsPlus
(877) 873-2085
www.wildbloomsplus.com

THE SLAUGHTEROUS RED RHODODENDRONS
Shepherd Hill Farm
200 Peekskill Hollow Rd.
Putnam Valley, NY 10579
(914) 528-5917

Carlson's Gardens
Box 305
South Salem, NY 10590
(914) 763-5958
www.carlsonsgardens.com

THE HUMBLE CROCUS
White Flower Farm
Route 63 Box 50
Litchfield, CT 06759-0050
(800) 503-9624
www.whiteflowerfarm.com

Schipper & Co.
PO Box 7584
Greenwich, CT 06836-7584
(800) 877-8637
www.colorblends.com

Eliot, *The Mill on the Floss*
WICKED WITH ROSES
Roseraie at Bayfields
PO Box R (wb)
Waldoboro, ME 04572-0919
(207) 832-6330
www.roseraie.com

Edmund's Roses
6235 SW Kahle Rd.
Wilsonville, OR 97070
(888) 481-ROSE
www.edmundsroses.com

Falkner, *Moonfleet*
THE ANCIENT QUINCE
Raintree Nursery
390 Butts Rd.
Morton, WA 98356
(360) 496-6400
www.raintreenursery.com

Hidden Springs Nursery
170 Hidden Springs Lane
Cookeville, TN 38501
(616) 268-9889

THE FORGOTTEN FIG
  The Fig Tree Nursery
  PO Box 124
  Gulf Hammock, FL 32639
  (904) 486-2930

  Edible Landscaping
  PO Box 77
  Afton, VA 22920
  (800) 524-4156
  www.eat-it.com

Fitzgerald, *Tender Is the Night*
NICOLE DIVER'S SUMMER GARDEN
  Smith & Hawken
  www.smith-hawken.com

  White Flower Farm
  Route 63, Box 50
  Litchfield, CT 06759-0050
  (800) 503-9624
  www.whiteflowerfarm.com

KALEIDOSCOPIC PEONIES
  Smirnow's Sons Peonies
  168 Maple Hill Rd. Dept HM
  Huntington, NY 11743
  (516) 421-0836

  The New Peony Farm
  PO Box 18235
  St. Paul, MN 55118
  (612) 457-8994

Forster, *Howards End*
THE DOG ROSES
  Heirloom Old Garden Roses
  24062 NE Riverside Dr.
  St. Paul, OR 97137
  (503) 538-1576

Forster, *Where Angels Fear to Tread*
THE PEA PATCH
  Johnny's Selected Seeds
  Foss Hill Rd.
  Albion, ME 04910-9371
  (207) 437-9294
  www.johnnyseeds.com

  Liberty Seed Company
  461 Robinson Drive SE
  New Philadelphia, OH 44663-0808
  (800) 541-6022
  www.libertyseed.com

Hawthorne, *The Blithedale Romance*
CLEVERLY CLIMBING VINES
  Conley's Garden Center
  145 Townsend Ave.
  Boothbay Harbor, ME 04538
  (800) 334-1812

  Heronswood Nursery
  7530 NE 288th St.
  Kingston, WA 98346-9502
  (360) 297-4172
  www.heronswood.com

Hawthorne, "Rappaccini's Daughter"
GARDEN ORNAMENT AND SCULPTURE
  Kenneth Lynch & Sons
  PO Box 488
  Wilton, CT 06897
  (203) 762-8363
  www.klynchandsons.com

  New England Garden Ornaments
  PO Box 235
  North Brookfield, MA 01535
  (508) 867-4475
  www.negardenornaments.com

SHOWY SHRUBS
Shepherd Hill Farm
200 Peekskill Hollow Rd.
Putnam Valley, NY 10579
(914) 528-5917

Fox Hill Nursery
347 Lunt Rd.
Freeport, ME 04032
(207) 729-1511

Holmes, *Elsie Venner: A Romance of Destiny*
FRAGRANT BOX
American Boxwood Society
Box 85
Boyce, VA 22620
(703) 939-4646

The Cummins Garden
22 Robertsville Rd.
Marlboro, NJ 07746
(908) 536-2591

THE SINGLE POPLAR
Cold Stream Farm
2030 Free Soil Rd.
Freesoil, MI 49411
(616) 464-5809

Hugo, *Les Misérables*
THE HEYDAY OF GILLYFLOWERS
Select Seeds Antique Flowers
180 Stickney Hill Rd.
Union, CT 06076-4617
(860) 684-9310
www.selectseeds.com

Lawrence, *Sons and Lovers*
SWOONING BEFORE LILIES
Cascade Valley Farms
Box 387
Parkdale, OR 97041
(888) 340-7098
www.cascadevalleyfarms.com

Dutch Gardens
PO Box 200
Adelphia, NJ 07710-0200
(800) 818-3861
www.dutchgardens.com

A TAPESTRY OF WHITE PHLOX
Dutch Gardens
PO Box 200
Adelphia, NJ 07710-0200
(800) 818-3861
www.dutchgardens.com

Avant Gardens
710 High Hill Rd.
Dartmouth, MA 02747
(508) 998-8819
www.avantgardensne.com

Mansfield, "Bliss"
A LOVELY PEAR TREE
Miller Nurseries
5060 West Lake Rd.
Canandaigua, NY 14424
(716) 396-2647
www.millernurseries.com

Adams County Nursery Inc.
PO Box 108
Aspers, PA 17304
(717) 677-8105

Proust, *Remembrance of Things Past:*
   Swann's Way
THE FLOWERING ALTAR
   Forestfarm
   900 Tetherow Rd.
   Williams, OR 97544-9599
   (541) 846-7269
   www.forestfarm.com

Sandburg, "How to Tell Corn Fairies If You See 'Em"
THE CORN FAIRIES' DANCE
   Johnny's Selected Seeds
   Foss Hill Rd.
   Albion, ME 04910-9371
   (207) 437-9294
   www.johnnyseeds.com

   Stokes Seeds, Inc.
   Box 548
   Buffalo, NY 14240-0548
   (716) 695-6980
   www.stokeseeds.com

Stowe, *Uncle Tom's Cabin*
AN INDULGENT CORNER OF ANNUALS
   W. Atlee Burpee Company
   300 Park Ave.
   Warminster, PA 18974
   (800) 888-1447
   http://garden.burpee.com

   Select Seeds Antique Flowers
   180 Stickney Hill Rd.
   Union, CT 06076-4617
   (860) 684-9310
   www.selectseeds.com

RASPBERRIES
   Brittingham Plant Farms
   PO Box 2538, Dept. GN96
   Salisbury, MD 21802-2538
   (410) 749-5153

   Nourse Farms, Inc.
   41 River Rd.
   Deerfield, MA 01373
   (413) 665-2658
   www.noursefarms.com

A SCARLET BEGONIA
   Antonelli Brothers, Inc.
   2545 Capitola Rd.
   Santa Cruz, CA 95062
   (888) 4-BEGONIAS
   www.infopoint.com/sc/market/antonelli

Trollope, *The Small House at Allington*
CROQUET AND OTHER VIGOROUS LAWN GAMES
   Oakley Woods Croquet
   (613) 475-3541
   www.oakleywoods.com

   San Diego Badminton Supply
   2571 South Coast Highway 101
   Cardiff by the Sea, CA 92007
   (760) 436-1404
   www.badminton.net

MISS LILY DALE'S PERFECT LAWN
   Seedland, Inc.
   www.seedland.com

Turgenev, *On the Eve*

THE CONTEMPLATIVE SHADE GARDEN
Shady Oaks Nursery
112 10th Ave. SE
Waseca, MN 56093
(800) 504-8006
www.shadyoaks.com

White Oak Nursery
6145 Oak Point Court
Peoria, IL 61614-3531
(309) 693-1354
www.whiteoaknursery.com

Twain, *The Adventures of Huckleberry Finn*

FACING THE SUN
Southern Exposure Seed Exchange
PO Box 170
Earlysville, VA 22936
(804) 973-4703
www.southernexposure.com
www.virtualseeds.com

Wharton, *Ethan Frome*

TRAVELER'S JOY
Completely Clematis
217 Arguilla Rd.
Ipswich, MA 01938-2617
(508) 356-3197
www.clematisnursery.com

Arthur H. Steffen, Inc.
PO Box 184
Fairport, NY 14450
(716) 377-1665

Wharton, *The House of Mirth*

THE LINGERING SUMMER GARDEN
Bluestone Perennials
7201 Middle Ridge
Madison, OH 44057
(216) 428-7535
www.bluestoneperennials.com

Garden.com, Inc.
3301 Steck Ave.
Austin, TX 78757
(800) 466-8142
www.garden.com

Wiggin, *Rebecca of Sunnybrook Farm*

GARDEN OF BUTTERCUPS
www.virtualseeds.com

Wilde, "Devoted Friend"

SHEPHERD'S PURSE AND OTHER
QUIRKY FLOWERS OF YESTERDAY
Select Seeds Antique Flowers
180 Stickney Hill Rd.
Union, CT 06076-4617
(860) 684-9310
www.selectseeds.com

Good Seed Co.
PO Box 1485
Tonasket, WA 98855
(509) 486-1047
www.planettonasket.com/GoodSeed

Wilde, *The Picture of Dorian Gray*
LANGUOROUS LILAC
  Fox Hill Nursery
  347 Lunt Rd.
  Freeport, ME 04032
  (207) 729-1511

  Wedge Nursery
  Route 2, Box 114
  Albert Lea, MN 56007
  (507) 373-5225

Zola, *Nana*
THE KITCHEN GARDEN
  Ferry-Morse Seed Company
  PO Box 488
  Fulton, KY 42041-0488
  (800) 283-2700
  www.ferry-morse.com

  Park Seed Company
  1 Parkton Ave.
  Greenwood, SC 29647-0001
  (800) 845-3369
  www.parkseed.com

ARTICHOKES!
  Pinetree Garden Seeds
  PO Box 300
  New Gloucester, ME 04260
  (207) 926-3400
  www.superseeds.com

  Shepherd's Garden Seeds
  30 Irene St.
  Torrington, CT 06790-6658
  (860) 482-3638
  www.shepherdseeds.com

A STRAWBERRY JAR
  Gardener's Supply Company
  128 Intervale Rd.
  Burlington, VT 05401-2850
  (800) 863-1700
  www.gardeners.com

❧ INDEX ❧

❧ ACKNOWLEDGMENTS ❧

THE FOLKS AT Lark Productions gratefully acknowledge the contribution of Duncan Brine. Tremendous appreciation and thanks go to illustrators Lea Richardson and Jesse Kaplan, and to Rachel Hoyt, Linda Holden, and Suzanne Herel. Thanks also to Ann Weinerman, who has a great nose for gardens in literature.

Duncan Brine is a landscape designer who worked in theater and film before founding his residential design firm, Horticultural Design, in 1984. Princeton-educated and raised in a family of critics and writers, he lives with his own family in upstate New York.